1 Enoch

1 Enoch

The Hermeneia Translation

George W. E. Nickelsburg
and
James C. VanderKam

Fortress Press
Minneapolis

1 ENOCH
The Hermeneia Translation

Cover art: Photograph of 4QEn^c i 6 (PAM 43. 199), a Qumran manuscript of the Aramaic of 1 Enoch 13–14. See J. T. Milik, *The Books of Enoch: Aramaic Fragments of Qumrân Cave 4* (Oxford: Clarendon, 1976), plate XII. For Milik's reconstruction of the text and its translation, see ibid., pp. 192–94. Photo reproduced by permission of the Israel Antiquities Authority.

Cover design: Ivy Palmer Skrade
Interior design: The HK Scriptorium

Library of Congress Cataloging-in-Publication Data

Ethiopic book of Enoch. English.
   1 Enoch : the Hermeneia translation / George W. E. Nickelsburg and James C. VanderKam.
      p. cm.
   Includes bibliographical references.
   ISBN 0-8006-3694-5 (alk. paper)
   I. Title: One Enoch. II. Title: First Enoch. III. Nickelsburg, George W. E., 1934- IV. VanderKam, James C. V. Title.
   BS1830.E6A3 2004b
   229' .913—dc22

                                                                2004015048

The paper used in this publication meets the minimum requirements of American National Standard for Information Sciences — Permanence of Paper for Printed Library Materials, ANSI Z329.48-1984.

Manufactured in the U.S.A.

Contents

Preface

1 Enoch is a collection of apocalyptic (revelatory) texts that were composed between the late fourth century B.C.E. and the turn of the era. The size of the collection, the diversity of its contents, and its many implications for the study of ancient Judaism and Christian origins make it arguably the most important Jewish writing that has survived from the Greco-Roman period.

In this revised edition, we offer a translation that is based on a critical reading of all the ancient textual sources. In chapters 37–82, it has been modified slightly from the first edition of this book (*1 Enoch: A New Translation* [Fortress Press, 2004]), and the whole is substantially the same as what appears in our commentaries in the Hermeneia commentary series, *1 Enoch 1* and *1 Enoch 2*. The translation in chapters 1–71 and 83–108 was prepared by George Nickelsburg, and that of chapters 72–82 by James VanderKam. The two of us are responsible for the parts of the introduction that pertain to the sections that we have translated. A bibliography provides resources for further study.

We wish to thank the editorial board of Hermeneia—A Critical and Historical Commentary on the Bible for their kind permission to publish our translation here in a separate format, and Fortress Press (facilitated by Neil Elliott, acquiring editor) for agreeing to print the revised edition. We are happy to acknowledge the fine work of Maurya Horgan and Paul Kobelski at the HK Scriptorium in designing and producing this work. We are also grateful to Sarah Schreiber for her help in proofreading the manuscript.

George W. E. Nickelsburg   James C. VanderKam
The University of Iowa   The University of Notre Dame

Abbreviations and Sigla

Abbreviations

Aram	Aramaic
chap.	chapter
Copt	Coptic
Eth	Ethiopic
frg.	fragment
Gk	Greek
Gk^a	Akhmim manuscript of the Greek version
Gk^s	Extracts of the Greek version quoted by the chronographer George Syncellus
hmt.	homoioteleuton, that is, words or lines that end with the same or similar letters or words
lit.	literally
ms(s)	manuscript(s)
NT	New Testament
Syr	Syriac
v(v)	verse(s)

Sigla Relating to the Translation and Its Textual Base

( )	Words supplied to clarify the translation. Also occasionally they indicate a parenthetical comment within the text itself.
< >	Textual emendation, either changing extant words or adding others presumed to have been lost
{ }	Words that are possibly not original
[ ]	Words supplied to fill a physical lacuna in a manuscript
††	Enclosed word(s) presumed to be corrupt
. . . .	A series of more than three periods indicates that a piece of text has been lost.

Chapter and verse numbers in boldface type indicate text that has been transposed from its place in the manuscripts.

Introduction

Contents of 1 Enoch

1 Enoch divides into five major sections, which are followed by two short appendices: The Book of the Watchers (chaps. 1–36); The Book of Parables (chaps. 37–71); The Book of the Luminaries (chaps. 72–82); The Dream Visions (chaps. 83–90); The Epistle of Enoch (chaps. 91–105); The Birth of Noah (chaps. 106–107); Another Book by Enoch (chap. 108). The sections represent developing stages of the Enochic tradition, each one building on the earlier ones—though not in the order in which they presently stand in the collection. Overall they express a common worldview that characterizes this present world and age as evil and unjust and in need of divine adjudication and renewal. With the possible exception of the Book of the Luminaries, they focus on the common concern and expectation that a coming divine judgment will eradicate evil and injustice from the earth and will return the world to God's created intention. Their authority lies in their claim that they transmit divine revelation, which the patriarch Enoch received in primordial times (Gen 5:21-24) and which is made public in the last times to constitute the eschatological community of the chosen.

The Book of the Watchers (Chaps. 1–36)

Chapters 1–5 were composed as an introduction to chapters 1–36, but now set the keynote for the entire work. They constitute a tri-partite prophetic oracle, in which "Enoch" announces the coming theophany, when God and the heavenly entourage will render judgment against the rebel angels who introduced evil into the world and against sinful humans, who perpetrate it. The first section (1:1-9) paraphrases part of Moses' final blessing on Israel (Deuteronomy 33) and an oracle of Balaam (Numbers 24) and bases Enoch's authority

1

on visions received in heaven and interpreted by angels. The second section (2:1—5:4), cast in the language of Israelite wisdom traditions, expands the indictment of "all flesh" (1:9) by contrasting the obedience of the heavenly bodies and the earthly seasons with humanity's disobedience. The final section (5:5-9) employs language from Isaiah 56–66 to describe the blessings and curses that await the righteous chosen and the sinners.

Chapters 6–11 are an interpretation of Genesis 6–9 that identifies events of the primordial past with those of the author's time. "The sons of God" (Gen 6:2), identified as angels ("watchers"), led by their chieftain Shemihazah, rebel against God by mating with mortal women and begetting giants, who devastate the earth. The giants can be interpreted as stand-ins for the warriors of the author's own time (the Hellenistic kings). The Genesis description of the Flood flows into a scenario that is appropriate for God's eschatological judgment and the inception of the new age. Interwoven with the myth of the watchers and the women is a second pair of myths, which identify the sin of the watchers as the revelation of forbidden secrets (metallurgy and mining, magic and the mantic arts) that promote violence and promiscuity. Here the rebel chieftain is Asael, a figure who resembles Prometheus, the rebellious divine figure of Greek myth. Humanity's plea, heard by the four high angels, triggers the judgment. With the sinful principals annihilated, a new age ensues with blessings for the chosen and those of humanity who have converted to the worship of God.

Chapters 12–16 interpret chapters 6–11, employing the form of a prophetic commissioning account. Enoch ascends to heaven, where God commands him to announce judgment on the fallen watchers. Here the watchers' sin is described as the forbidden intermixture of flesh and spirit. Different from chapters 6–11, the death of the watchers does not annihilate them, but releases their spirits to constitute a realm of evil spirits who plague humanity until the final judgment.

Chapters 17–32 enhance the account of Enoch's commissioning by providing a spatial reference to the previous temporal prediction of a future judgment. Enoch sees *the places* where the apparatus of judgment has been prepared and where it will be executed. Chapters 17–19 recount Enoch's journey to the far northwest, where in the company of interpreting angels, he views the places of final punishment for the watchers and certain rebellious stars. Chapters 20–32 describe a second journey, which begins where the first one left off and carries Enoch across the face of the earth to its eastern reaches. Here, in addition to the places described in the previous journey, Enoch recounts his visions of the places of eschatological significance *for humanity*—both the righteous chosen and the sinners (the place of the dead, the mountain of God, and Jerusalem), as well as primordial Eden. As in the previous journey, the literary form of the segments of this journey includes these elements: Enoch's progress to a new place; his vision; his question; an interpretation by the accompanying angel. The account of Enoch's journey to the places of the luminaries (chaps. 33–36) briefly summarizes material in chapters 72–82. The Book of the Watchers probably took its present form by the mid- or late third century B.C.E.

The Book of Parables (Chaps. 37–71)

These chapters of 1 Enoch were originally a separate Enochic writing that announced the coming of the great judgment, in which God would vindicate the "chosen and righteous" and punish their oppressors, "the kings and the mighty." The book divides into three major sections called "parables" or "similitudes" (chaps. 38–44; 45–57; 58–69). The term here reflects the usage of biblical prophetic literature and denotes a revelatory discourse. Since the expression occurs also in 1 Enoch 1:2-3 and 93:1, 3 (Aramaic), it is less distinctive of chapters 37–71 than the universal scholarly designation "the Book of Parables" might indicate. In fact, the author's introduction entitles the work Enoch's "vision of wisdom" (37:1).

Running through the parables are four major types of material, three of which parallel other parts of 1 Enoch. The book as a whole depicts a series of journeys. The seer ascends to the heavenly throne room (39:3—41:2). Then he visits the astronomical and other celestial phenomena (chaps. 41–44; 59–60) and the places of punishment (especially 52:1—56:4). The second set of materials includes narratives about Noah and the Flood (especially chaps. 65–68). As in chapters 6–11 and 106–107 the Flood is a type of the final judgment. The third group of materials consists of a series of heavenly tableaux, scenes in a developing drama that depicts events leading up to the final judgment.

Intermingled with these tableaux is a series of anticipatory allusions to the judgment, often introduced with the words "in those days."

The drama depicted in the Parables includes a diverse cast of characters. On the one side are God, God's heavenly entourage, the agents of divine judgment (primarily "the Chosen One," but also certain of God's angels), and God's people ("the chosen," "the righteous," and "the holy"). On the other side are the chief demon Azazel, his angels, and the kings and the mighty. God is usually called "the Lord of Spirits," a paraphrase of the biblical title "Lord of Hosts," or "the Head of Days" (cf. Dan 7:9). The Chosen One combines the titles, attributes, and functions of the one like a son of man in Daniel 7:13-14, the Servant of the Lord in Second Isaiah, the Davidic Messiah, and pre-existent heavenly Wisdom (Proverbs 8). Although "son of man" is a Semitic way of saying "human being," the usage in Daniel 8:15; 9:21; 10:5; 12:6 indicates that an angel can be called "a/the man" or described as having "the appearance of a man." The Chosen One is the agent of God's judgment and as such is depicted with imagery that the early chapters of 1 Enoch ascribe to God. Related to his judicial function is his role as the champion of God's people, and his titles "the Chosen One" and "the Righteous One" correspond to the titles "the chosen" and "the righteous ones." The salient features of God's people are their status as God's chosen ones, their righteousness, their suffering, and their faith in God's vindication. Azazel and his hosts are the counterparts of Asael and of Shemihazah and his hosts (chaps. 6–11), and their major sin here is the revelation of secrets. "The kings and the mighty," the real villains of the piece, deny the name of the Lord of Spirits and the heavenly world, worship idols, and oppress and persecute the righteous.

The first parable introduces most of the dramatis personae, as well as the theme of judgment. Together with the introduction to the book (chap. 37), it follows roughly the structure of the first chapters of 1 Enoch. (Compare chap. 37 with 1:1-3; chap. 38 with 1:3-9; 39:1 with chaps. 6–11; and 39:2-14; 40 with chap. 14.) The Wisdom poem in chapter 42 suggests a parody on Sirach 24 and Baruch 3:9—4:4. Wisdom does not dwell in Israel; unrighteousness drove her back to heaven—a pithy summary of the apocalyptic worldview (cf. 94:5).

In the second parable, chapters 46–47 present the first tableau in the developing drama about the Chosen One and the judgment. In 46:1-3 the author draws on Daniel 7:9, 13, identifying his protagonist with the one like a son of man in Daniel 7. The tableau in chapters 48–49 depicts the naming of "that son of man" through an interpretation of the call of the Servant in Isaiah 49. Language about the preexistence of that son of man and his name (vv 3, 6) suggests that this figure is related to preexistent Wisdom. The unique expression "kings of the earth" and the reference to "the Lord of Spirits and his Anointed" (48:8, 10) are drawn from Psalm 2:2 and reflect biblical language about the Davidic Messiah, as does the paraphrase of the royal oracle in Isaiah 11:2 at 49:3. Verse 4 paraphrases Isaiah 42:1, the source of the Servant title "the Chosen One." Chapters 50–51 anticipate future events connected with the judgment, and 51:4-5 designates earth as the locus of salvation and eternal life (cf. 45:4-6). The journey and visions described in chapters 52:1—56:4 are related to the myth of the angels and to the journey traditions in 1 Enoch 6–11 and 17–21.

The third parable focuses on the great judgment itself. The climactic tableau in chapters 62–63 employs a traditional judgment scene, attested also in Wisdom of Solomon 4–5. The present text begins with the exaltation of the Chosen One (a Servant title). The kings and the mighty who stand before him are the counterpart of the audience in Isaiah 52–53. Verse 2 draws on the language of Isaiah 11:2, 4, the messianic strand of the Chosen One tradition (cf. 49:3). The kings and the mighty petition for mercy without success and are driven from the presence of the Lord and delivered to the angels of punishment (62:9-12; cf. 53:3-5). The author then shifts the focus to the righteous and chosen and to their coming deliverance and fellowship with their helper and champion, the son of man (62:13-16; cf. Isa 52:1). Chapter 63 is the counterpart of the confession in Isaiah 53:1-6.

Chapters 65–68 are a collection of Noachic traditions. The story in chapter 65 is closely related to 1 Enoch 83–84 and 106–107 and presumes a typology between the Flood and the last judgment. The scene in 69:26-29 belongs with the judgment scene in chapters 62–63.

The Book of Parables in its present form has two conclusions. The first briefly recounts Enoch's final removal from earth (70:1-2). The second (70:3—71:17) is Enoch's own summarizing account of his removal to Paradise and his ascent to heaven, where instead of being commissioned to be a prophet of judgment (chaps. 14–16) he is presented as "the son of man who was born for righteousness" (71:14; cf. 46:1-3).

The Parables can be dated sometime around the turn of the era.

The reference to the Parthians and the Medes in 56:5 may refer to the invasion in 40 B.C.E., just before the beginning of the reign of Herod the Great. At the very least, the description of the Chosen One/son of man (if not the entire book) is presumed in the gospel traditions about Jesus, the Son of Man.

The Book of the Luminaries (Chaps. 72–82)

Enoch, whose biblical age at his final removal by God was 365 years, naturally became associated with the annual calendar. The Book of the Luminaries is the place where these traditions are recorded. It contains the revelations that the angel Uriel (his name means "God is my light") showed to Enoch about these subjects when the two of them were together. Like the other early Enoch texts, it was written in the Aramaic language, four copies of which have been found at Qumran (see below, pp. 96–115). The evidence of the Aramaic manuscripts indicates that the original work was much longer than the form that has survived in the Ethiopic translation. In its Aramaic form, the book seems to have begun, after an introduction setting the scene, with a long section in which the movements of the sun and moon were synchronized for perhaps a one-year period, with the lunar data receiving the larger amount of attention. It then continued with material about winds and the gates through which they emerge, various geographical subjects, and the return of Enoch to earth. The Aramaic copies also show that the original form of the book contained a description of the four leaders of the luminaries. Since the earliest copy of the Book of the Luminaries dates from about 200–150 B.C.E., the work may have been composed in the third century B.C.E., possibly earlier. It may therefore be the oldest Enochic composition.

The long Aramaic form of the book was translated into Greek, though only a few fragments of the version are available. The most complete surviving text is the Ethiopic translation of the Greek; in it the original length of the astronomical work is significantly abbreviated. It begins by saying that Uriel revealed these matters to Enoch (72:1) and then immediately gives the law of the great light, the sun; included is the amount of time each day that it is light and dark (understanding a day to be divided into 18 units) over a one-year period of 364 days. There are 12 months of 30 days each, with one extra day in the third, sixth, ninth, and twelfth months. The sun rises through six gates in the east and sets through six gates in the west; it moves from gate to gate, switching each month in its annual progression (72:2-37). The moon, which also moves through these gates, is the subject of 73:1—74:9, while 74:10-17 compare a solar year of 364 days and a lunar one of 354 days. The subject of gates in the heavens is very important in 75:1—76:14; the winds emerge from sets of three gates situated in each of the cardinal points of the compass. This geographical notice precedes a section in which other statements about the earth appear (the four quarters, seven mountains, seven rivers, seven islands [77:1-8]). Chapter 78 reverts to the sun and moon. It seems that chapter 79 sets the stage for the completion of the book, since in it Enoch addresses his son Methuselah and tells him that the revelation about the law of the stars is complete. Related contents may be found in 81:1—82:9. Here he is told to pass along the information to his son Methuselah with whom he is to stay for one year before his final removal. The last part of the book (82:10-20) claims it will speak of the four leaders who divide the four seasons, but after two are treated (vv 15-17, 18-20) the text breaks off.

One section that stands out from the others and could be an addition is 80:2-8 which speaks of the days of the sinners when the years will be shorter, crops and the moon will not appear at the right times, stars will go astray, and sinners will deify them. This section stands in tension with the rest of the book which presupposes unchanging patterns for the luminaries and speaks of sinners only in connection with those who fail to reckon the four extra days in a solar year. This is the only part of the Book of the Luminaries that has an eschatological focus (although see the end of 72:1), while the remainder of the book is mainly descriptive of what the writer understands to be the workings of the luminaries and the arrangement of the world that God had created. It is possible that chapter 81 is also an editorial insertion that aligns the Book of the Luminaries with other parts of 1 Enoch.

In these revelations to Enoch there are two calendars: a solar year of 364 days and a lunar year of 354 days. This information also appears in calendrical texts from Qumran, but, unlike those texts, the Book of the Luminaries never mentions the Jewish festivals or the sabbath and thus does not date them according to either of these calendars. The combination of calendrical and geographical contents in the book may be a reflection of astrological traditions in which heavenly signs or omens were thought to predict happenings in certain parts of the earth.

The Dream Visions (Chaps. 83–90)

Enoch recounts two dream visions about future events. In the first he foresees the world's destruction in the Flood (chaps. 83–84). In its literary line and its typology of Flood and final judgment, the narrative in chapter 83 parallels stories about Noah in chapters 65 and 106–107, and the prayer in chapter 84 is probably dependent on the angelic prayer in chapter 9.

In his second dream vision (chaps. 85–90), Enoch sees the history of the world played out in allegorical form. Human beings are depicted as animals, the sinful angels as fallen stars, and the seven archangels as human beings.

The first of three major eras runs from creation to the first judgment in the Flood (85:3—89:58). All the human dramatis personae are cattle. For his account of the events described in Genesis 6:1-4 (chaps. 86–88), the author has drawn heavily on the traditions in chapters 6–11. The first star to fall is Asael (86:1-3; 88:1; cf. 1 Enoch 10:4). Other stars descend from heaven, become bulls, and mate with the heifers (i.e., women), thus producing camels, elephants, and asses (i.e., the giants, 86:3-6). The era ends with God's judgment in the Flood.

The second era begins with the renewal of creation after the Flood. Noah, a white bull, and his three sons, a white, a red, and a black bull (89:9), correspond to Adam and his three sons, who were depicted in the same way (85:3, 8). After Noah's death, the menagerie begins to diversify, signifying a differentiation between the patriarchs of Israel and the Gentiles. From the red and black bulls (Ham and Japheth), many species of animals and fowl arise, all of them unclean by Jewish standards and many of them predators. From Shem's line come Abraham and Isaac, white bulls like himself. Isaac begets a black wild boar (Esau, the patriarch of the hated Edomites) and a white sheep (Jacob, the patriarch of the tribes of Israel, 89:10-12).

The image of Israel as sheep has two biblical nuances. (1) The sheep are often blinded and go astray; that is, that nation is guilty of unbelief and apostasy (89:32-33, 41, 51-54, 74; 90:7). (2) The Israelite sheep are the victims of the wild beasts that represent the Gentiles, often as divine punishment for their apostasy (89:13-21, 42, 55-57; 90:2-4, 11-13, 16).

Israel's mounting apostasy leads to a new turn in the nation's history.

Around the time of Manasseh (89:54-58), the Lord of the sheep appoints seventy angelic shepherds to pasture the sheep until the end-time (89:59-64), each on duty for a specified period of time (89:64; 90:5).

The return from Exile does not improve matters. Although the temple is rebuilt, all its sacrifices are polluted, and the sheep are blinded (89:73-74). During the Seleucid rule (after 198 B.C.E.), a time of unmitigated violence, some of the younger generation (the pious Jews) open their eyes and appeal to the older ones (in part, the Hellenizers) to return from their wickedness, but to no avail (90:6-8). The parallels between vv 9b-10, 12-16 and 6-9a, 11, 17-19 indicate either duplicate versions of the same block of text or an updating of the original text of the vision. In the present form of the vision, the action centers around the ram with a great horn, namely, Judas Maccabeus.

The historical section of the vision concludes with a theophany (90:18), and a threefold judgment against the rebel angels (v 24; cf. 10:4-6, 11-13), the disobedient shepherds (v 25), and the apostate Jews (vv 26-27; cf. 10:14).

With the judgment complete, the third and final era of human history begins. God constructs a new Jerusalem (90:28-29). The Gentiles come to pay homage to the Jews (v 30). The dispersed people of God return, and the dead are raised (v 33). Then a great white bull is born and all the beasts and birds are transformed into his likeness. Thus the end-time reverts to the primordial time of creation. The distinction between Jew and Gentile is obliterated (cf. 10:21). Israel's victimization at the hands of the Gentiles has ceased. With no red and black cattle in the wings, the situation is permanent.

In its present form, the vision dates from the time of Judas Maccabeus (between 164 and 160 B.C.E.), although the parallel passages in 90:6-19 may indicate an earlier date around 200 B.C.E. It was composed among people who considered the Second Temple to be polluted and who understood themselves to be the eschatological community of the righteous constituted by a claim to revelation (90:6).

The Epistle of Enoch with an Introduction (Chaps. 91–105)

Chapter 91 is a piece of testamentary instruction, in which Enoch, on the eve of his final departure from the earth, summons his sons and admonishes them to lead the right life. His idiom is that of the two ways, typical of biblical and post-biblical wisdom literature. Verses 5-9 are a schematic summary of human history that emphasizes how God executes judgment (both at the Flood and at the end-time) against those who have followed the path of wrong conduct. The chapter as a whole, which begins with an admonition to Methuselah, recalls the testamentary instruction in 81:1—82:3, an alien body that is now embedded in the Book of the Luminaries.

This testamentary setting provides the context for the Epistle itself (chaps. 92–105), which, as a whole, constitutes ethical instruction and threats and promises that are based on Enoch's visions, which have been recorded in the earlier parts of the corpus. Although the Epistle is ostensibly addressed to Enoch's children, mentioned in chapter 91, it is in fact directed to the author's own contemporaries, "the future generations that will practice righteousness and peace" (92:1; cf. 1:1-2; 37:2). On the basis of his revealed knowledge of the heavenly realm, Enoch assures his readers that God's imminent judgment will bring vindication and everlasting blessing to the righteous and swift punishment to their powerful oppressors. Thus, although the times are troubled, he can exhort the righteous to faith, steadfastness, and joy.

Following the introduction (chap. 92), Enoch recites the Apocalypse of Weeks (93:1-10 + 91:11-17) on the basis of a threefold appeal to revelation (93:2). The ancient sage summarizes world history from his time to the eschaton, employing a scheme of ten periods of uneven length called "weeks." The historical survey focuses on "the chosen of eternity" and "the plant of righteousness" (93:2). Initially this metaphor refers to Israel, sprung from Abraham (93:5). Running through the apocalypse is the counter-motif of wickedness, often construed as violence, deceit, and apostasy (93:4, 8, 9; 91:11 [Aramaic]). These are met by God's judgment in the Flood and the Exile. History climaxes in the seventh week, the author's own time. The plant of righteousness has been pruned to an elect remnant, the author's community, which is endowed with revealed, sevenfold (complete) wisdom, that is, the contents of the author's message and probably the rest of the Enochic corpus. They will function as "witnesses of righteousness" and will uproot the counter-structure of deceit (93:10 Aramaic). In the eighth, ninth, and tenth weeks, judgment will be executed against their oppressors, all the grossly wicked, and the fallen angels (91:12-

15). Remaining humanity will convert to righteousness (91:14; cf. 10:21). God will purge the earth of evil and renew the heavens and its luminaries (91:16-17). A prose section following the apocalypse meditates on the uniqueness of the revelation granted Enoch and now shared by the author's community (93:11-14). A few verses of two-ways instruction (94:1-5) serve as a bridge to the main section of the epistle, which spells out (by condemnation) the way of wickedness followed by "the sinners" and encourages "the righteous" to be steadfast in the hope of vindication. This central part of the epistle is composed almost entirely of three literary forms well known from the biblical tradition, especially from the prophets. All three carry the theme of the coming judgment.

The woes juxtapose in their two major components the paradox of historical injustice and belief in divine judgment. Collectively the indictments in these woes provide a description of the author's world. The charges are of two types. The first are religious, strictly speaking: idolatry (99:7), consuming blood (98:11), blasphemy (94:9; 96:7), cursing (95:4), disregarding and perverting divine law as the righteous ("the wise") understand it (99:2; 98:9; 99:14), thus leading many astray (98:15). The second type of woe attributes social misdeeds to the sinners. The rich and powerful abuse the righteous, build sumptuous houses at the expense of others (94:6-7; 99:13), banquet in luxury while the poor suffer (96:5-6), hoard wealth and food (97:8-9), parade about in fine clothes and jewelry (98:1-3), and perjure themselves (95:6).

The exhortations embody the same paradox as the woes. In their first part some of them call the righteous to courage, faith, and hope in view of the sinners' coming judgment described in the second part. Other exhortations appeal for courage in the face of present calamity (first part) on the basis of a promise of vindication and everlasting life for the righteous (second part):

Descriptions of the judgment or events leading up to it constitute the third major form in these chapters. The adverbial introductions ("then" or "in those days") recall parallel passages in the prophetic books.

The author's use of prophetic forms suggests that he is presenting his message as revelation, an impression strengthened by his use of formulas that elsewhere introduce revelations and especially forecasts: "Know!" "Be it known!" "I say to you." Stronger yet is the oath formula "I swear to you." References to happenings in the heavenly realm also presume Enoch's claim to revelation (97:6; 98:6-8; 103:1-4; 104:1, 7-8).

The main section of the epistle reaches its climax in 102:4—104:8, which takes the form of a dispute about the existence or nonexistence of retribution, that is, the judgment that has been the epistle's main subject. In each of the four parts of this dispute the author addresses a particular group, quotes certain words about or by them, and then refutes these words with an appeal to revelation.

The epistle closes with explicit reference to the transmission of Enoch's teaching. In the end-time his books will be given to the righteous (cf. 93:10) and will be a source of wisdom, faith, and joy (104:12-13), and they will serve as a testimony to the children of earth (105:1-2). With this reference to the future generation, the paths of righteousness, and the peace that belongs to the righteous, the author returns to the themes of his superscription (92:1).

The Epistle dates from the second century B.C.E. and was added as a conclusion to the corpus before both the Book of Parables and the Book of the Luminaries were incorporated into the collection.

The Birth of Noah (Chaps. 106–107)

According to this narrative, Noah's miraculous birth foreshadowed his role as the preserver of the human race. Placed at the end of the corpus, the story promises salvation for the righteous, who will survive the great judgment that was prefigured in the Flood. As a literary type, the story parallels accounts of special births in the Hebrew Bible (e.g., Isaac, Samson, and Samuel) as well as the stories of the conceptions of Jesus and John the Baptist in Matthew 1 and Luke 1. Its structure also parallels 1 Enoch 65 and 83.

A Final Book of Enoch (Chap. 108)

This "other book that Enoch wrote" is actually a summarizing and interpretive conclusion to the corpus, which exhorts the righteous who live "in the end of days" to endure in their expectation because the judgment will soon vindicate them and eradicate sin and the sinners who have troubled and oppressed them. The author draws on ideas, expressions, and traditions that will resonate with the reader of the earlier chapters and creates a conclusion that interprets the corpus as a revelation of eschatological import that is intended to console and exhort.

Translation

The components of 1 Enoch were composed in Aramaic and then translated into Greek, and from Greek into ancient Ethiopic (*Geʿez*). The entire collection is extant only in manuscripts of the Ethiopic Bible, of which this text is a part. Approximately ninety such manuscripts from the fifteenth to the twentieth centuries are available to scholars in the West. We have consulted nearly fifty of these. Roughly twenty-five percent of 1 Enoch has survived in two Greek manuscripts from the fourth and fifth/sixth centuries (chaps 1:1—32:6; 97:6—107:3) and a few fragments of other parts. Eleven manuscripts from Qumran contain substantial as well as tiny fragments of the Aramaic of parts of chapters 1–36, 72–82, 85–90, and 91–107. A fragment of a sixth/seventh-century Coptic manuscript (93:3-8), an extract in a ninth-century Latin manuscript (106:1-18), and a twelfth-century Syriac excerpt (6:1-6) have also survived.[1]

Of necessity, the Ethiopic version is our base text, although we have used the Greek where it is available and provides better readings and gives a better sense of the original Aramaic. We have systematically consulted the Aramaic; however, the fragmentary state of these manuscripts, which contain few whole sentences, makes it difficult to employ them in a sustained way. We have also referred to the fragmentary Coptic, Latin, and Syriac evidence.

The textual evidence that supports our translation has been presented in the apparatuses in Nickelsburg, *1 Enoch 1,* and Nickelsburg and VanderKam, *1 Enoch 2.* In addition, for comparative purposes VanderKam translates here the relevant parts of the Qumran Aramaic texts of the Book of the Luminaries.

---

1. For details on all the textual evidence, see Nickelsburg, *1 Enoch 1,* 9–20.

In a few places, where literary considerations seem to warrant it, George Nickelsburg has transposed some lines or verses (18:12-16; 41:3-8; 47:2c; 51:5a; 54:2; 60:11-23; 65:4, 9; 89:49; 91:11-17; 100:2e). Where a textual emendation seemed warranted, we have given a brief explanation in a note.

The translation seeks to balance a literal rendering of the original with readable English style. To this end, with a broader audience in view, George Nickelsburg has made some revisions of the translation in his commentary.[2] Large parts of chapters 1–36, 83–84, and 91–108 have been set in the parallelistic poetic format that is evident in the text, although the details of such formatting are open to discussion.[3]

Bibliography

Bautch, Kelley Coblentz. *A Study of the Geography of 1 Enoch 17–19: "No One Has Seen What I Have Seen."* Journal for the Study of Judaism Supplements 81. Leiden: Brill, 2003.
  Translation, text-critical notes, and discussion.
Beyer, Klaus. *Die aramäischen Texte vom Toten Meer.* Göttingen: Vandenhoeck & Ruprecht, 1984.
  Transcription of Qumran Aramaic Fragments.
Black, Matthew. *The Book of Enoch or 1 Enoch: A New English Edition with Commentary and Notes, in Consultation with James C. VanderKam, with an Appendix on the 'Astronomical' Chapters (72–82) by Otto Neugebauer.* Studia in Veteris Testamenti Pseudepigrapha 7. Leiden: Brill, 1985.
Bonner, Campbell, ed. *The Last Chapters of Enoch in Greek.* London: Christophers, 1937. Stuttgart: Wissenschaftliche Buchgesellschaft, 1968 reprint.
  Edition of Greek papyrus of 1 Enoch 97–107.

---

2. On the principles of that translation, see ibid., 19.
3. Ibid., 35–36.

Charles, R. H. *The Book of Enoch or 1 Enoch.* Oxford: Clarendon, 1912. Introduction, translation, and commentary. Second edition of ground-breaking English-language work. Translation and abbreviated annotation appeared in his edition of *The Apocrypha and Pseudepigrapha of the Old Testament,* 2:163–281. 2 vols. Oxford: Clarendon, 1913.

Charles, R. H. *The Ethiopic Version of the Book of Enoch: Edited from Twenty-Three MSS. Together with the Fragmentary Greek and Latin Versions.* Anecdota Oxoniensia, Semitic Series 11. Oxford: Clarendon, 1906. Critical edition of Ethiopic version and text of Greek version of 1 Enoch 1–32.

Chesnutt, Randall. "*Oxyrhynchus Papyrus* 2069 and the Compositional History of *1 Enoch,*" *JBL* 129 (2010) 485–505.

Chialà, Sabino. *Libro delle parabole di Enoc.* Studi Biblici 117. Brescia: Paideia, 1997. Introduction, translation, and commentary on the Book of Parables.

Drawnel, Henryk. *The* Aramaic Astronomical Book (Oxford and New York: Oxford University Press, 2011).

Isaac, Ephraim. "1 (Ethiopic Apocalypse of) Enoch." In James H. Charlesworth, ed., *The Old Testament Pseudepigrapha,* 1:5–89. 2 vols. Garden City: Doubleday, 1983–85. Translation of one Ethiopic manuscript with textual apparatus.

Knibb, Michael A. *The Ethiopic Book of Enoch: A New Edition in the Light of the Aramaic Dead Sea Fragments: In Consultation with Edward Ullendorff.* 2 vols. Oxford: Clarendon, 1978. Text and translation of one Ethiopic manuscript, with full critical apparatus of Ethiopic manuscripts and reference to Aramaic fragments and Greek texts.

Larson, Erik. "The Translation of Enoch: From Aramaic into Greek." Dissertation. New York University, 1995. Detailed comparative analysis of the Qumran Aramaic fragments and the corresponding parts of the Greek translation.

Milik, J. T. *The Books of Enoch: Aramaic Fragments of Qumrân Cave 4.* Oxford: Clarendon, 1976. Edition and translation of Qumran Aramaic fragments and detailed introduction and comments.

Nickelsburg, George W. E. *1 Enoch 1: A Commentary on the Book of 1 Enoch, Chapters 1–36; 81–108.* Hermeneia. Minneapolis: Fortress Press, 2001.

Extended introduction, translation and critical apparatus, and detailed critical commentary on all of 1 Enoch except the Book of Parables and Book of the Luminaries.

Nickelsburg, George W. E. *Jewish Literature Between the Bible and the Mishnah: A Historical and Literary Introduction.* Second edition. Minneapolis: Fortress Press, 2005.

Introduction to the various parts of 1 Enoch.

Nickelsburg, George W. E. "Son of Man." In *Anchor Bible Dictionary,* 6:137–50. Edited by D. N. Freedman. New York: Doubleday, 1992.

Son of man in the Hebrew Bible, 1 Enoch, and the New Testament.

Nickelsburg, George W. E., and James C. VanderKam. *1 Enoch 2: A Commentary on the Book of 1 Enoch, Chapters 37–82.* Hermeneia: Minneapolis: Fortress Press, 2011.

Olson, Daniel C. *Enoch: A New Translation. The Ethiopic Book of Enoch, or 1 Enoch Translated with Annotations and Cross References in Consultation with Archbishop Melkesedek Workeneh.* North Richmond Hills, Tex.: Bibal, 2004.

Stuckenbruck, Loren T. *1 Enoch 91–108.* CEJL. Berlin and New York: de Gruyter, 2007.

Tigchelaar, E. J. C. and F. Garcia Martinez. "4QAstronomical Enoch[a-b]." In *Qumran Cave 4* vol. 26, 95–172. Discoveries in the Judaean Desert 36. Oxford: Clarendon, 2000.

Fragments of two Aramaic manuscripts related to 1 Enoch 72–82.

Tiller, Patrick A. *A Commentary on the Animal Apocalypse of 1 Enoch.* Society of Biblical Literature Early Judaism and its Literature Series 4. Atlanta: Scholars, 1993.

Commentary on 1 Enoch 85–90.

Uhlig, Siegbert. *Das Äthiopische Henochbuch.* Jüdische Schriften aus hellenistisch-römischer Zeit 5/6. Gütersloh: Mohn, 1984.

Introduction, translation, and notes.

VanderKam, James C. "1 Enoch, Enochic Motifs, and Enoch in Early Christian Literature." In James C. VanderKam and William Adler, eds., *The Jewish Apocalyptic Heritage in Early Christianity,* 33–101.

Compendia Rerum Iudaicarum ad Novum Testamentum 3.4. Minneapolis: Fortress Press, 1996.

VanderKam, James C. *Calendars in the Dead Sea Scrolls: Measuring Time*. New York: Routledge, 1998.

Study of Qumran calendars related to the Book of the Luminaries.

VanderKam, James C. *Enoch: A Man for All Generations.* Studies on Personalities of the Old Testament. Columbia, S.C.: University of South Carolina Press, 1995.

The figure of Enoch in Jewish and Christian literature.

VanderKam, James C. *Enoch and the Growth of an Apocalyptic Tradition.* Catholic Biblical Quarterly Monograph Series 16. Washington, D.C.: Catholic Biblical Association of America, 1984.

The Enochic corpus and its background especially in Mesopotamian texts.

VanderKam, James C. *An Introduction to Early Judaism.* Grand Rapids: Eerdmans, 2001.

The Book of the Watchers

(Chapters 1–36)

Superscription to the Book

1:1   THE WORDS OF THE BLESSING WITH WHICH ENOCH BLESSED THE RIGHTEOUS CHOSEN who will be present on the day of tribulation, to remove all the enemies; and the righteous will be saved.

Introduction: An Oracle of Judgment (1:2—5:9)

2   And he took up his discourse[a] and said,
     "Enoch, a righteous man whose eyes were opened by God,
         who had the vision of the Holy One and of heaven, which
             he showed me.
     From the words of the watchers and holy ones I heard every-
         thing;
         and as I heard everything from them, I also understood
             what I saw.
     Not for this generation do I expound,
         but concerning one that is distant I speak.
3   And concerning the chosen I speak now,
         and concerning them I take up my discourse.

The Theophany

     "The Great Holy One will come forth from his dwelling,
4   and the eternal God will tread from thence upon Mount
         Sinai.

---

a Lit. *parable* (Aram *matla'*: Gk *parabolē*).

He will appear with his army,[a]
> he will appear with his mighty host from the heaven of
> heavens.

5 All the watchers will fear and <quake>,[b]
> and those who are hiding in all the ends of the earth will
> sing.

All the ends of the earth will be shaken,
> and trembling and great fear will seize them (the watchers)
> unto the ends of the earth.

6 The high mountains will be shaken and fall and break apart,
> and the high hills will be made low and melt like wax
> before the fire.

7 The earth will be wholly rent asunder,
> and everything on the earth will perish,
> and there will be judgment on all.

8 With the righteous he will make peace,
> and over the chosen there will be protection,
> and upon them will be mercy.

They will all be God's,
> and he will grant them his good pleasure.[c]

He will bless (them) all,
> and he will help (them) all.

Light will shine upon them,
> and he will make peace with them.

9 Look, he comes with the myriads of his holy ones,
> to execute judgment on all,
> and to destroy all the wicked,
> and to convict all humanity
>> for all the wicked deeds that they have done,
>> and the proud and hard words that wicked sinners
>> spoke against him.

---

a Eth: Gk *from his camp* (same Gk noun).

b Eth *all will fear and the watchers will quake*: Gk *all will fear and the watchers will believe*.

c Gk *good pleasure* (*eudokian*): Eth *prosperity* (=Gk *euodian*).

The Indictment[a]

2:1   "Contemplate all (his) works, and observe the works of heaven, how they do not alter their paths; and the luminaries <of>[b] heaven, that they all rise and set, each one ordered in its appointed time; and they appear on their feasts and do not transgress their own appointed order.

2   Observe the earth, and contemplate the works that take place on it from the beginning until the consummation, that nothing on earth changes, but all the works of God are manifest to you.

3   Observe <the signs of summer and winter. Contemplate the signs of>[c] winter, that all the earth is filled with water, and clouds and dew and rain rest upon it.

3:1   Contemplate and observe how all the trees appear withered and (how) all their leaves are stripped, except fourteen trees that are not stripped, which remain with the old until the new comes after two or three years.

4:1   Observe the signs of summer, whereby the sun burns and scorches, and you seek shelter and shade from its presence, and the earth burns with scorching heat, and you are unable to tread on the dust or the rock because of the burning.

5:1   Contemplate all the trees; their leaves blossom green on them, and they cover the trees. And all their fruit is for glorious honor.
      Contemplate all these works, and understand that he who lives for all the ages made all these works. 2/ And his works take place from year to year, and they all carry out their works for him, and their works do not alter, but they all carry out his word.

3   Observe how, in like manner, the sea and the rivers carry out and do not alter their works from his words.

---

a The textual witnesses in this section are often at odds with one another, frequently because of omissions in one or another. For details, see Nickelsburg, *1 Enoch 1*, 150–51.

b Gk Eth *in.*

c Text of this section uncertain. For the rationale of this emendation, see *1 Enoch 1*, 150.

4   But you have not stood firm nor acted according to his
                commandments;
             but you have turned aside, you have spoken proud and
                hard words with your unclean mouth against his
                majesty.
         Hard of heart! There will be no peace for you!

The Verdict

5   "Then[a] you will curse your days, and the years of your life
                will perish,
             and the years of your destruction will increase in an
                eternal curse;
             and there will be no mercy or peace for you!
6   Then you will leave your names as an eternal curse for all the
                righteous,
             and by you all who curse will curse,
             and all the sinners and wicked will swear by you.[b]
         But all the <chosen>[c] will rejoice;
             and for them there will be forgiveness of sins and all mercy
                and peace and clemency.
         For them there will be salvation, a good light,
             and they will inherit the earth.[d]
         But for all you sinners there will be no salvation,
             but on all of you a curse will abide.
7   For the chosen there will be light and joy[e] and peace,
             and they will inherit the earth.
             But for you wicked there will be a curse.[f]

8   Then wisdom will be given to all the chosen;
             and they will all live,
             and they will sin no more through godlessness or pride.

---

a Aram: Gk Eth *therefore*.
b Eth omits the rest of this verse.
c Gk corrupt for *sinners*. Emendation by analogy with v 7a.
d Distich closely parallels v 7ab and could be a doublet.
e Eth (=Gk *chara*): Gk *grace* (*charis*).
f Gk adds a veritable doublet of v 7ab.

> In the enlightened man there will be light,
>> and in the wise man, understanding.[a]
> And they will transgress no more,
>> nor will they sin[b] all the days of their life,

9
>> nor will they die in the heat of <God's> wrath.[c]
> But the number of the days of their life they will complete,
>> and their life will grow in peace,
>> and the years of their joy will increase in rejoicing and
>>> eternal peace
> all the days of their life."

The Rebellion of the Watchers (Chapters 6–11)

The Conspiracy

6:1   When the sons of men[d] had multiplied, in those days, beautiful and comely daughters were born to them. 2/ And the watchers, the sons of heaven, saw them and desired them.[e] And they said to one another, "Come, let us choose for ourselves wives from the daughters of men,[f] and let us beget children for ourselves."

3   And Shemihazah, their chief, said to them, "I fear that you will not want to do this deed, and I alone shall be guilty of a great sin."

---

a For the distich Eth has *but those who have wisdom will be humble.*

b Eth *nor will they be judged.*

c Emending Gk to *en orgē thymou <theou>* positing an omitted word.

d Language about "sons of God," "sons of men," and "daughters of men" in these chapters reflects Gen 6:1-4, on which this myth is based. We might translate "sons of God" as "heavenly beings," "sons of men" as "humans" or "human men," and "daughters of men" as "human women." However, to retain the complex relationships among these terms, to indicate gender distinctions where they are evident, and to avoid the confusion that would arise from the partial replacement of the terms, it seems best to translate the text literally in this section, reminding the reader that this is a story about the illicit mating of beings from the divine and the human realms.

e Gk[s] adds *and went astray after them*: Syr adds *and went astray.*

f Gk[s] Syr add *of earth.*

4   And they all answered him and said, "Let us all swear an oath, and let us all bind one another with a curse, that none of us turn back from this counsel until we fulfill it and do this deed."

5   Then they all swore together and bound one another with a curse. 6/ And they were, all of them, two hundred, who descended in the days of Jared onto the peak of Mount Hermon. And they called the mountain "Hermon" because they swore and bound one another with a curse on it.

7   And these are the names of their chiefs:[a] Shemihazah—this one was their leader; Arteqoph, second to him; Remashel, third to him; Kokabel, fourth to him; <Armumahel>, fifth to him; Ramel, sixth to him; Daniel, seventh to him; Ziqel, eighth to him; Baraqel, ninth to him; Asael, tenth to him; Hermani, eleventh to him; Matarel, twelfth to him; Ananel, thirteenth to him; Setawel, fourteenth to him; Samshiel, fifteenth to him; Sahriel, sixteenth to him; <Tummiel>, seventeenth to him; Turiel, eighteenth to him; Yamiel, nineteenth to him; Yehadiel, twentieth to him. 8/ These are their chiefs of tens.[b]

The Deed and Its Results

7:1   These and all the others with them took for themselves wives from among them such as they chose.[c] And they began to go in to them, and to defile themselves through them, and to teach them sorcery and charms, and to reveal to them the cutting of roots and plants.

2   And they conceived from them and bore to them great giants. And the giants begot Nephilim, and to the Nephilim were born †Elioud†. And they were growing in accordance with their greatness.

---

a The angelic names, which are often corrupted in the Gk and Eth, are largely attested in the Aram. For these and the emendations made here, see 1 Enoch 1, 175.

b The original wording of this verse is uncertain. See 1 Enoch 1, 175.

c For the textual problems in this chapter, see 1 Enoch 1, 182–83.

3   They were devouring the labor of all the sons of men,[a] and
        men were not able to supply them. 4/ And the giants began
        to kill men and to devour them. 5/ And they began to sin
        against the birds and beasts and creeping things and the fish,
        and to devour one another's flesh. And they drank the blood.
6   Then the earth brought accusation against the lawless ones.

The Secrets the Watchers Reveal[b]

8:1   Asael taught men to make swords of iron and weapons and
        shields and breastplates and every instrument of war.
        He showed them metals of the earth and how they should
        work gold to fashion it suitably, and concerning silver, to
        fashion it for bracelets and ornaments for women. And he
        showed them concerning antimony and eye paint and all
        manner of precious stones and dyes.
        And the sons of men made them for themselves and for their
        daughters, and they transgressed and led the holy ones
        astray.[c] 2/ And there was much godlessness on the earth, and
        they made their ways desolate.
3   Shemihazah taught spells and the cutting of roots.
        Hermani taught sorcery for the loosing of spells and magic
        and skill.
        Baraqel taught the signs of the lightning flashes.
        Kokabel taught the signs of the stars.
        Ziqel taught the signs of the shooting stars.
        Arteqoph taught the signs of the earth.
        Shamsiel taught the signs of the sun.
        Sahriel taught the signs of the moon.

---

a Aram fragment attests *sons of men*: Gk[a], as often, has only *men*. This single word
has been left in the translation in its next two occurrences and elsewhere in these chapters where no Aram exists.

b Translation of this chapter is based on a fairly certain resolution of very complex
textual data. See *1 Enoch 1*, 188–90.

c Gk[a] Eth omit this sentence, attested in Gk[s]. It reflects a form of the myth in
which the angelic revelations are primary and lead to the seduction of the holy ones.
Cf. 10:8.

And they all began to reveal mysteries to their wives and to
their children.[a]

4   (And) as men were perishing, the cry went up to heaven.

The Intercession of the Four Archangels

9:1   Then Michael and Sariel[b] and Raphael and Gabriel looked
         down from the sanctuary of heaven upon the earth and saw
         much bloodshed on the earth. All the earth was filled with
         the godlessness and violence that had befallen it.

2   And entering in, they said to one another, "The earth, devoid
         (of inhabitants), raises the voice of their cries to the gates of
         heaven. 3/ And now to <us>, the holy ones of heaven, the
         souls of men make suit, saying,
         'Bring in our judgment to the Most High,
            and our destruction before the glory of the majesty,
            before the Lord of all lords in majesty.'"

4   And approaching, they said to the Lord of the Ages,
         "You are the God of gods and Lord of lords and King of
            kings and God of the ages.
            And the throne of your glory (exists) for every generation
               of the generations that are from of old.
            And your name (is) holy and great and blessed for all the
               ages.

5   For you have made all things and have authority over all.
            And all things are manifest and uncovered before you,
            and you see all things, and there is nothing that can be
               hidden from you.

6   You see what Asael has done,
         who has taught all iniquity on the earth,
            and has revealed the eternal mysteries that are in heaven,
            <which the sons of men were striving to learn.>[c]

---

a Sentence attested in Gk[s], supported by Aram.

b For this name, attested in Aram, Gk has forms of *Uriel* (*ouriēl/ouēl*) and Eth
sureʾēl/sureyāl, probably reflecting a Gk confusion of *sigma* and *omicron*. For the textual
evidence on this chapter, see *1 Enoch 1*, 202–5.

c All textual witnesses of this line are corrupt. For emendation, see *1 Enoch 1*, 204.

7   And (what) Shemihazah (has done) to whom you gave
           authority to rule over them who are with him.
8   They have gone in to the daughters of the men of earth,
           and they have lain with them, and have defiled themselves
               with the women.
           And they have revealed to them all sins, and have taught
               them to make hate-inducing charms.
9   And now look, the daughters of men have borne sons from
           them, giants, half-breeds.
           <And the blood of men is shed on the earth,>^a[a]
           And the whole earth is filled with iniquity.
10   And now look, the spirits of the souls of the men who have
           died make suit,
           and their groan has come up to the gates of heaven,
           and it <does not cease>[b] to come forth from the presence
               of the iniquities that have come upon the earth.
11   You know all things before they happen,
           and you see these things and you permit them,
           and you do not tell us what we ought to do to them with
               regard to these things."

The Commissioning of the Four Archangels

Sariel Commissioned to Instruct Noah

10:1   Then the Most High declared, and the Great Holy One
           spoke.
           And he sent <Sariel>[c] to the son of Lamech, saying,
2   "Go to Noah and say to him in my name, 'Hide yourself.'
           And reveal to him that the end is coming, that the whole
               earth will perish;
           and tell him that a deluge is about to come on the whole
               earth and destroy everything on the earth.
3   Teach the righteous one what he should do,
           the son of Lamech how he may preserve himself alive and
               escape forever.

---

a Line attested only in Gk^s, which is corrupt. See *1 Enoch 1*, 204.

b Positing an Aram corruption from *does not cease* to *is unable* (Gk Eth).

c Name emended to match 9:1.

From him a plant will be planted,
  and his seed will endure for all the generations of
    eternity."[a]

Raphael Commissioned to Imprison Asael

4   To Raphael he said,
      "Go, Raphael, and bind Asael hand and foot, and cast him
        into the darkness;
      And make an opening in the wilderness that is in
        Doudael.[b]
5   Throw him there, and lay beneath him[c] sharp and jagged
        stones.
      And cover him with darkness, and let him dwell there for
        an exceedingly long time.
      Cover up his face, and let him not see the light.
6   And on the day of the great judgment, he will be led away
            to the burning conflagration.
7   And heal the earth, which the watchers have desolated;
          and announce the healing of the earth, that the plague
            may be healed,
          and all the sons of men may not perish because of the
            mystery that the watchers told and taught their sons.
8   And all the earth was made desolate by the deeds of the
            teaching of Asael,
          and over him[d] write all the sins."

---

a The translation of Aram ʿalam and its Gk and Eth equivalents is problematic. No single English translation is satisfactory. Normally, it is translated *eternity* and in its adjectival form *eternal*. Here the plural is translated *ages*, and the singular is rendered *eternity*, which better conveys the immense time than does *the age*. For the adjective, *everlasting* seems better to convey the notion of an extended time than *eternal*, although this latter is used with reference to the Deity. The ʿalam is thought of as consisting of an everlasting sequence of periods (alternatively *all the ages* or *all the days* [or *generations*] *of eternity*). When ʿalam follows a preposition, the noun is rendered *from of old* or *forever* or *for an exceedingly long time* where appropriate (cf. 10:5 with 10:6). No English word indicates the fact that in the Greco-Roman period ʿalam is acquiring spatial as well as temporal connections (*world* as well as *age*).

b Gkˢ Eth: Gkᵃ: *Dadouēl*. See *1 Enoch 1*, 222.

c Eth *over him*.

d Or *concerning him*.

Gabriel Commissioned to Destroy the Giants

9   And to Gabriel he said,
     "Go, Gabriel, to the bastards, to the half-breeds, to the sons
          of miscegenation;
       and destroy the sons of the watchers from among the sons
          of men;
       send them against one another in a war of destruction.
     Length of days they will not have;
10   and no petition will be (granted) to their fathers in their
          behalf,
       that they should expect to live an everlasting life, nor even
          that each of them should live five hundred years."

Michael Commissioned to Imprison Shemihazah
and his Associates and to Destroy the Giants[a]

11   And to Michael he said,
     "Go, Michael, bind Shemihazah and the others with him, who
     have mated with the daughters of men, so that they were
     defiled by them in their uncleanness.
12   And when their sons perish and they see the destruction of
     their beloved ones, bind them for seventy generations in
     the valleys of the earth, until the day of their judgment and
     consummation, until the everlasting judgment is consum-
     mated.
13   Then they will be led away to the fiery abyss, and to the tor-
     ture, and to the prison where they will be confined forever.
14   And everyone who is condemned and destroyed henceforth
     will be bound together with them until the consummation
     of their generation. <And at the time of the judgment, which
     I shall judge, they will perish for all generations.>
15   Destroy all the spirits of the half-breeds and the sons of the
     watchers, because they have wronged men.

---

a For the textual problems of this section, see *1 Enoch 1*, 217–19.

Michael Is to Renovate the Earth

16   Destroy all perversity from the face of the earth,
          and let every wicked deed be gone;
          and let the plant of righteousness and truth^a appear, and it
              will become a blessing,
              (and) the deeds of righteousness and truth will be planted
              forever with joy.
17   And now all the righteous will escape,
          and they will live until they beget thousands,
          and all the days of their youth and their old age will be
              completed in peace.
18   Then all the earth will be tilled in righteousness,
          and all of it will be planted with trees and filled with
              blessing;
19   and all the trees of joy will be planted on it.
      They will plant vines on it,
          and every vine that will be planted on it will yield a
              thousand jugs of wine,
          and of every seed that is sown on it, each measure will
              yield a thousand measures,
          and each measure of olives will yield ten baths of oil.
20   Cleanse the earth from all impurity and from all wrong and
              from all lawlessness and from all sin,
          and godlessness and all impurities that have come upon
              the earth, remove.
21   And all the sons of men will become righteous,
          and all the peoples will worship (me),
          and all will bless me and prostrate themselves.
22   And all the earth will be cleansed from all defilement and
              from all uncleanness,
          and I shall not again send upon them any wrath or
              scourge for all the generations of eternity.

---

a These two nouns here and in the next line may be double translations of Aram
qushta᾽.

11:1   Then I shall open the storehouses of blessing that are in
           heaven,
              and make them descend upon the earth, upon the works
              and the labor of the sons of men.
2   And then truth and peace will be united together
           for all the days of eternity and for all the generations of
           humanity."

Enoch's Interaction with the Fallen Watchers (Chapters 12–16)

An Editorial Introduction

12:1   Before these things, Enoch was taken; and no human being[a]
           knew where he had been taken, or where he was, or what had
           happened to him.
2   His works were with the watchers,
           and with the holy ones were his days.

Enoch's First Mission to the Fallen Watchers

Enoch Is Sent to the Watchers

3   I, Enoch, was standing, blessing the Lord of majesty, the King
           of the ages. And look, the watchers of the Great Holy One
           called me, Enoch the scribe, and said to me,
4   "Enoch, righteous scribe, go and say to the watchers of
           heaven—who forsook the highest heaven, the sanctuary of
           the(ir) eternal station, and defiled themselves with women.
           As the sons of earth do, so they did and took wives for them-
           selves. And they worked great desolation on the earth—
           5/ 'You will have no peace or forgiveness.'
6   "And concerning their sons, in whom they rejoice—

---

   a Lit. *none of the sons of men.* This translation for the generic term is adopted hereafter where feasible.

The slaughter of their beloved ones they will see,
    and over the destruction of their sons they will lament and
        make perpetual petition,
    and they will have no mercy or peace.

Enoch Is Sent to Asael

13:1   "And, Enoch, go and say to Asael,
    'You will have no peace.
        A great sentence has gone forth against you, to bind you.
2   You will have no relief or petition,
        because of the unrighteous deeds that you revealed,
        {and because of all the godless deeds and the unrighteous-
           ness and the sin that you revealed to humans.'"}[a]
3   Then I went and spoke to all of them together.
    And they were all afraid,
        and trembling and fear seized them.

The Fallen Watchers Commission Enoch
to Intercede for Them

4   And they asked that I write a memorandum of petition for
them, that they might have forgiveness, and that I recite the
memorandum of petition for them in the presence of the
Lord of heaven. 5/ For they were no longer able to speak
or to lift their eyes to heaven out of shame for the deeds
through which they had sinned and for which they had
been condemned. 6/ Then I wrote out the memorandum of
their petition, and the requests concerning themselves, with
regard to their deeds individually, and concerning <their
sons> for whom they were making request, that they might
have forgiveness and longevity. 7/ And I went off and sat
by the waters of Dan in the land of Dan, which is south of
Hermon, to the west. I recited (to God) the memorandum of
their petition until I fell asleep.

---

a Bracketed passage appears to be an expanded doublet of the previous line.

Enoch's Ascent to Heaven and
Second Commission to Preach to the Watchers

Narrative Summary

8   And look, dreams came upon me, and visions fell upon me.
       And I saw visions of wrath, and there came a voice, saying,
       "Speak to the sons of heaven to reprimand them." 9/ And
       when I had awakened, I went to them. And all of them were
       assembled together, and they were sitting and weeping at Abel-
       Main,[a] which is between Lebanon and Senir, covering their
       faces. 10/ And I recited in their presence all the visions that I
       had seen in the dream, and I began to speak the words of truth
       and the vision and reprimand to the watchers of heaven.

The Commission Summarized

14:1   THE BOOK OF THE WORDS OF TRUTH AND THE REPRIMAND
       OF THE WATCHERS WHO WERE FROM OF OLD, according to
       the command of the Great Holy One <in the dream that
       I dreamed>.[b] 2/ In this vision I saw in my dream what I
       now speak with a human tongue and with the breath of my
       mouth, which the Great One has given to humans, to speak
       with them and to understand with the heart. 3/ As he created
       and destined humans to understand the words of knowledge,
       so he created and destined me[c] to reprimand the watchers,
       the sons of heaven.

4   I wrote up your petition, and in the vision it was shown to
               me thus,
           that you will not obtain your petition for all the days of
               eternity;
               but judgment has been consummated in the decree against
                   you,

---

a For these place names and the text of v 10, see *1 Enoch 1*, 248–50.

b Bracketed words, omitted in Gk and Eth, supplied from Aram. See *1 Enoch 1*,
251.

c For this clause Aram reads *he destined and made and created me.*

5   that from now on you will not ascend into heaven for all the
           ages;
       and it has been decreed to bind you in bonds in the earth
           for all the days of eternity.
6   And that before these things, you will see the destruction of
           your sons, your beloved ones,
       and that you will have no pleasure in them,
       but they will fall before you by the sword.[a]
7   Accordingly, you will not obtain your petition concerning
           them, nor concerning yourselves.
       You will be petitioning and making supplication;
           . . . but you will not be speaking any word from the writ-
               ing that I have written.[b]

Enoch's Ascent and Vision

8   In the vision it was shown to me thus:
       Look, clouds in the vision were summoning me, and mists
           were crying out to me;
           and shooting stars and lightning flashes were hastening me
               and speeding me along,
           and winds in my vision made me fly up and lifted me
               upward and brought me to heaven.
9   And I went in until I drew near to a wall built of hailstones;
           and tongues of fire were encircling them all around,
           and they began to frighten me.
10   And I went into the tongues of fire, and I drew near to a
           great house built of hailstones;
           and the walls of this house were like stone slabs,
           and they were all of snow, and the floor was of snow.
11   And the ceiling was like shooting stars and lightning flashes;
           and among them were fiery cherubim, and their heaven
               was water,
12   and a flaming fire encircled all their walls, and the doors
               blazed with fire.

---

a The text of this verse is problematic. See *1 Enoch 1*, 251–52.

b The text of this verse is also problematic and perhaps missing a line. See *1 Enoch 1*, 252–53.

13   And I went into that house—hot as fire and cold as snow,
          and no delight of life was in it.
      Fear enveloped me, and trembling seized me,
14   and I was quaking and trembling, and I fell upon my face.
      And I saw in my vision,
15   And look, another open door before me:
          and a house greater than the former one,
          and it was all built of tongues of fire.
16   All of it so excelled in glory and splendor and majesty
          that I am unable to describe for you its glory and majesty.
17   Its floor was of fire,
          and its upper part was flashes of lightning and shooting
              stars,
          and its ceiling was a flaming fire.
18   And I was looking and I saw a lofty throne;
          and its appearance was like ice,
          and its wheels were like the shining sun,
          and †the voice (*or* sound) of†[a] the cherubim,
19   and from beneath the throne issued rivers of flaming fire.
      And I was unable to see.
20   The Great Glory sat upon it;
          his apparel was like the appearance of the sun
          and whiter than much snow.
21   No angel could enter into this house and look at his face
          because of the splendor and glory,
          and no human could look at him.
22   Flaming fire encircled him and a great fire stood by him,
          and none of those about him approached him.
      Ten thousand times ten thousand stood before him,
          but he needed no counselor; his every word was deed.[b]

---

a Eth, which could reflect Ezek 10:5: Gk (*its*) *boundary was* (*horos*), perhaps suggesting the sides of the throne, or it may be a corruption of *choros* (choir). For other
alternatives, see *1 Enoch 1*, 258, 264.

b Gk omits first clause, and Eth, the second. Cf. 2 Enoch 33:4.

23   And the holy ones of the watchers[a] who approached him did
      not depart by night,
      nor <by day>[b] did they leave him.

The Oracle

24   Until now I had been on my face, prostrate and trembling.
And the Lord called me with his mouth and said to me,
"Come here, Enoch, and hear my word(s)." 25/ And one of
the holy ones came to me and raised me up and stood me (on
my feet) and brought me up to the door. But I had my face
bowed down.

15:1   But he answered and said to me—and I heard his voice—
      "Fear not, Enoch, righteous man and scribe of truth;
      come here, and hear my voice.

2   Go and say to the watchers of heaven, who sent you to
      petition in their behalf,
      'You should petition in behalf of humans,
      and not humans in behalf of you.

3   Why have you forsaken the high heaven, the eternal
      sanctuary;
      and lain with women, and defiled yourselves with the
      daughters of men;
      and taken for yourselves wives, and done as the sons of
      earth;
      and begotten for yourselves sons, giants?

4   You were holy ones and spirits, living forever.
With the blood of women you have defiled yourselves,
      and with the blood of flesh you have begotten,
and with the blood of men you have lusted,
      and you have done as they do—
      flesh and blood, who die and perish.

5   Therefore I gave them women,
      that they might cast seed into them,
      and thus beget children by them,
      that nothing fail them on the earth.

---

a For *watchers* Gk reads *angels*. For the reading see *1 Enoch 1*, 258.
b Conjectured phrase added to fill out parallelism. See *1 Enoch 1*, 259, 265–66.

6   But you originally existed as spirits, living forever,
      and not dying for all the generations of eternity;
7   therefore I did not make women among you.'
     The spirits of heaven, in heaven is their dwelling;
8   But now the giants who were begotten by the spirits and
      flesh—
     they will call them evil spirits on the earth,
     for their dwelling will be on the earth.
9   The spirits that have gone forth from the body of their flesh
      are evil spirits,
     for from humans[a] they came into being, and from the
      holy watchers was the origin of their creation.
     Evil spirits they will be on the earth, and evil spirits they
      will be called.
10   The spirits of heaven, in heaven is their dwelling;
     but the spirits begotten on the earth, on the earth is their
      dwelling.[b]
11   And the spirits of the giants <lead astray>, do violence, make
     desolate, and attack and wrestle and hurl upon the earth
     and <cause illnesses>. They eat nothing, but abstain from
     food and are thirsty and smite. 12/ These spirits (will) rise up
     against the sons of men and against the women, for they have
     come forth from them.
16:1   From the day of the slaughter and destruction and death of the
     giants, from the soul of whose flesh the spirits are proceed-
     ing, they are making desolate without (incurring) judgment.
     Thus they will make desolate until the day of the consum-
     mation of the great judgment, when the great age will be
     consummated. It will be consummated all at once.
2   And now (say) to the watchers who sent you to petition in
     their behalf, who formerly were in heaven,
3   'You were in heaven, and no mystery was revealed to you;
     but a stolen mystery you learned;

---

a Gk[s]: Gk[a] Eth *for from above.* One reading is a Gk corruption of the other. See *1 Enoch 1*, 268.

b For the textual problems and conjectures in the rest of this section, see *1 Enoch 1*, 268–69.

and this you made known to the women in your hardness
of heart;
and through this mystery the women and men are
multiplying evils on the earth.'

4   Say to them,
'You will have no peace.'"

Enoch's Journey to the Northwest (Chapters 17–19)

The Journey Narrative Begun

17:1   And they took me (and) led (me) away to a certain place in
       which those who were there were like a flaming fire; and
       whenever they wished, they appeared as human beings.

2   And they led me away to a dark place and to a mountain
       whose summit reached to heaven. 3/ And I saw the place
       of the luminaries and the treasuries of the stars and of the
       thunders, and to the depths of the ether, where the bow of
       fire and the arrows and their quivers (were) and the sword of
       fire[a] and all the lightnings.

4   And they led me away to the living waters and to the fire of the
       west, which provides[b] all the sunsets.

5   And I came to the river of fire, in which fire flows down like
       water and discharges into the great sea of the west. 6/ I saw
       all the great rivers.
       And I arrived at the great river and the great darkness.
       And I departed (for) where no human[c] walks. 7/ I saw the
       wintry winds of darkness and the gushing of all the waters of
       the abyss. 8/ I saw the mouth of all the rivers of the earth and
       the mouth of the abyss.

A Digression: A Summary of What Enoch Saw

18:1   I saw the treasuries of all the winds. I saw how through them
       he ordered all created things.

---

a Gk omits the phrase.

b Eth *receives.*

c Lit. *no flesh*, which could mean *no living being.*

2   I saw the foundation of the earth and the cornerstone of the
         earth. I saw the four winds bearing the earth and the firma-
         ment of heaven. 3/ And I saw how the winds stretch out the
         height of heaven. They stand between earth and heaven; they
         are the pillars of heaven.
4   I saw the winds of heaven that turn and bring to (their) setting
         the disk of the sun and all the stars.
5   I saw the winds on the earth bearing the clouds.
         I saw the paths of the angels.
         I saw at the ends of the earth the firmament of heaven above.

The Journey Narrative Concluded

6   I came and saw a place that was burning night and day, where
         (there were) seven mountains of precious stones—three lying
         to the east and three to the south. 7/ And of those to the east,
         (one was) of colored stone, and one was of pearl, and one was
         of <jasper>.ᵃ And those to the south were of flame-colored
         stone. 8/ And the middle one of them reached to heaven like
         the throne of God—of antimony; and the top of the throne
         was of lapis lazuli. 9/ And I saw a burning fire.
10   And beyond these mountains is a place, the edge of the great
         earth; there the heavens come to an end. 11/ And I saw a great
         chasm among pillars of heavenly fire. And I saw in it pillars
         of fire descending; and they were immeasurable toward the
         depth and toward the height.ᵇ
19:1   And Uriel said to me, "There stand the angels who mingled
         with the women. And their spirits—having assumed many
         forms—bring destruction on men and lead them astray to
         sacrifice to demons as to gods until the day of the great judg-
         ment, in which they will be judged with finality. 2/ And the
         wives of the transgressing angels will become sirens."

---

   a The identity of the stone is uncertain. See *1 Enoch 1*, 286.

   b As it is preserved, the text narrates Enoch's progress to two places, followed by
two angelic interpretations. Additionally, in Enoch's next journey, from west to east
(chaps. 21–32), the order of stations suggests the transposition here of 19:1-2 between
18:11 and 18:12. See *1 Enoch 1*, 287.

18:12   Beyond this chasm I saw a place where there was neither firmament of heaven above, nor firmly founded earth beneath
it. Neither was there water on it, nor bird; but the place was
desolate and fearful. 13/ There I saw seven stars like great
burning mountains.

14   To me, when I inquired about them, the angel said, "This
place is the end of heaven and earth; this has become a prison
for the stars and the hosts of heaven. 15/ The stars that are
rolling over in the fire, these are they that transgressed the
command of the Lord in the beginning of their rising, for
they did not come out in their appointed times. 16/ And he
was angry with them and bound them until the time of the
consummation of their sins—ten thousand years."

19:3   I, Enoch, alone saw the visions, the extremities of all things.
And no one among humans has seen as I saw.

Enoch's Journey Eastward (Chapters 20–36)

List of the Seven Archangels

20:1   These are the names of the holy angels who watch.

2   Uriel, one of the holy angels, who is in charge of the world and
Tartarus.

3   Raphael, one of the holy angels, who is in charge of the spirits
of men.

4   Reuel, one of the holy angels, who takes vengeance on the
world of the luminaries.

5   Michael, one of the holy angels, who has been put in charge of
the good ones of the people.[a]

6   Sariel, one of the holy angels, who is in charge of the spirits[b]
who sin against the spirit.

———————

a Textual witnesses are confused here. The verse may originally have ascribed to
Michael supervision over all of Israel or over the righteous of Israel. See *1 Enoch 1*,
294–96.

b Eth adds *of the sons of men.*

7   Gabriel, one of the holy angels, who is in charge of paradise
        and the serpents and the cherubim.
8   Remiel, one of the holy angels, whom God has put in charge
        of them that rise.
        The names of the seven archangels.[a]

The Place of Punishment for the Disobedient Stars

21:1   I traveled to where it was chaotic. 2/ And there I saw a terrible
        thing; I saw neither heaven above, nor firmly founded earth,
        but a chaotic and terrible place. 3/ And there I saw seven of
        the stars of heaven, bound and thrown in it together, like
        great mountains, and burning in fire.
4   Then I said, "For what reason have they been bound, and for
        what reason have they been thrown here?"
5   Then Uriel said to me, one of the holy angels who was with
        me, and he was their leader, he said to me, "Enoch, why do
        you inquire, and why are you eager for the truth? 6/ These
        are the stars of heaven that transgressed the command of the
        Lord; they have been bound here until ten thousand years are
        fulfilled—the time of their sins."

The Prison of the Fallen Angels

7   From there I traveled to another place, more terrible than this
        one. And I saw terrible things—a great fire burning and flam-
        ing there. And the place had a narrow cleft (extending) to the
        abyss, full of great pillars of fire, borne downward. Neither
        the measure nor the size was I able to see or to estimate.
8   Then I said, "How terrible is this place and fearful to look at!"
9   Then Uriel[b] answered me, one of the holy angels who was with
        me, and said to me, "Enoch, why are you so frightened and
        shaken?"

---

a Eth omits this verse.

b Gk omits the name. Perhaps it is a gloss. Cf. 19:1-2; 18:13, which have only one
name.

And I replied, "Because of this terrible place and because of the fearful sight."

10 And he said, "This place is a prison for the angels. Here they will be confined forever."

The Mountain of the Dead

22:1 From there I traveled to another place. And he showed me to the west a great and high mountain of hard rock. 2/ And there were four hollow places in it, deep and very smooth. Three of them were dark and one, illuminated; and a fountain of water was in the middle of it.

And I said, "How smooth are these hollows and altogether deep and dark to view."

3 Then Raphael answered me, one of the holy angels who was with me, and said to me, "These hollow places (are intended) that the spirits of the souls of the dead might be gathered into them. For this very (purpose) they were created, (that) here the souls of all human beings should be gathered. 4/ And look, these are the pits for the place of their confinement. Thus they were made until the day (on) which they will be judged, and until the time of the day of the end of the great judgment that will be exacted from them."

5 There I saw the spirit of a dead man making suit, and his lamentation went up to heaven and cried and made suit.

6 Then I asked Raphael, the watcher and holy one[a] who was with me, and said to him, "This spirit that makes suit—whose is it—that thus his lamentation goes up and makes suit unto heaven?"

7 And he answered me and said, "This is the spirit that went forth from Abel, whom Cain his brother murdered. And Abel

---

a Aram: Gk Eth *angel* suggesting that elsewhere in this section, where there are no Aram counterparts, *holy angel* may also have translated Aram *watcher(s) and holy one(s)*.

makes accusation against him until his posterity[a] perishes from the face of the earth, and his posterity is obliterated from the posterity of men."

8   Then I asked about all the hollow places, why they were separated one from the other.

9   And he answered me and said, "These three were made that the spirits of the dead might be separated.
And this has been separated for the spirits of the righteous, where the bright fountain of water is.

10 And this has been created for <the spirits of the> sinners, when they die and are buried in the earth, and judgment has not been executed on them in their life. 11/ Here their spirits are separated for this great torment, until the great day of judgment, of scourges and tortures of the cursed forever, that there might be a recompense for their spirits. There he will bind them forever.

12 And this has been separated for the spirits of them that make suit, who make disclosure about the destruction, when they were murdered in the days of the sinners.

13 And this was created for the spirits of the people who will not be pious, but sinners, who were godless, and they were companions with the lawless. And their spirits will not be punished on the day of judgment, nor will they be raised from there."

14 Then I blessed the Lord of glory and said, "Blessed is the judgment of righteousness and blessed are you, O Lord of majesty and righteousness, who are Lord of eternity."[b]

The Fire of the West

23:1 And from there I traveled to another place, to the west of the ends of the earth. 2/ And I saw a fire that ran and did not rest or quit its course day and night, but continued.

---

a   Lit. *seed.*

b   Textual witnesses to this verse differ. See *1 Enoch 1*, 301–2.

3   And I asked and said, "What is this that has no rest?"

4   Then Reuel answered me, one of the holy angels who was
        with me, and said to me, "This course of fire is the fire of
        the west, which pursues[a] all the luminaries of heaven."[b]
        24:1/ And he showed me mountains of fire that burned day
        and night.

The Mountain of God and the Tree of Life

24:2   And I proceeded beyond them, and I saw seven glorious
        mountains, all differing each from the other, whose stones
        were precious in beauty. And all (the mountains) were pre-
        cious and glorious and beautiful in appearance—three to the
        east were firmly set one on the other, and three to the south,
        one on the other, and deep and rugged ravines, one not
        approaching the other. 3/ The seventh mountain (was) in the
        middle of these, and it rose above them in height, like[c] the
        seat of a throne. And fragrant[d] trees encircled it. 4/ Among
        them was a tree such as I had never smelled, and among them
        was no other like it.[e] It had a fragrance sweeter smelling than
        all spices, and its leaves and its blossom and the tree[f] never
        wither. Its fruit is beautiful, like dates of the palm trees.

5   Then I said, "How beautiful is this tree and fragrant,[g] and its
        leaves are lovely, and its blossoms[h] are lovely to look at."

6   Then Michael answered me, one of the holy angels who
        was with me and was their leader, 25:1/ and he said to me,

---

  a Gk *to ekdiōkon*: Eth corrupt. However, cf. 20:4, which applies the verb *ekdeikōn*
(*takes vengeance on*) to *Reuel*. See *1 Enoch 1*, 310–11.

  b Eth adds a clause here that indicates Enoch's movement to a new place. See
1 Enoch 1, 311.

  c Text of previous clause uncertain. See *1 Enoch 1*, 312.

  d Eth (= Gk *euōdē*): Gk *beautiful to see* (*eueidē*).

  e On the text, see *1 Enoch 1*, 312.

  f Perhaps originally *and the blossom of the tree*.

  g Gk: Eth. *beautiful to see*. See above note h.

  h Eth *its fruit*.

"Enoch, why do you inquire and why do you marvel about the fragrance of this tree, and why do you wish to learn the truth?"

25:2   Then I answered him—I, Enoch—and said, "Concerning all things I wish to know, but especially concerning this tree."

3   And he answered me and said, "This high mountain that you saw, whose peak is like the throne of God, is the seat where the Great Holy One, the Lord of glory, the King of eternity, will sit, when he descends to visit the earth in goodness. 4/ And (as for) this fragrant tree, no flesh has the right to touch it until the great judgment, in which there will be vengeance on all and a consummation forever.

Then it will be given to the righteous and the pious,
5   and its fruit will be food for the chosen.
And it will be transplanted to the holy place,
          by the house of God, the King of eternity.
6   Then they will rejoice greatly and be glad,
          and they will enter into the sanctuary.
Its fragrances <will be>[a] in their bones,
          and they will live a long life on the earth,
          such as your fathers lived also in their days,[b]
          and torments and plagues and suffering will not touch them."

7   Then I blessed the God of glory, the King of eternity, who has prepared such things for people (who are) righteous, and has created them and promised to give (them) to them.

Jerusalem, the Center of the Earth and the Place of Punishment

26:1   And from there I proceeded to the center of the earth, and I saw a blessed place where there were trees that had branches that abide and sprout. 2/ And there I saw a holy mountain.

---

a Emending an evident corruption in Aram original, *1 Enoch 1*, 313.
b Eth adds *sorrow* at the beginning of the next line.

From beneath the mountain water (came) from the east, and it flowed toward the south. 3/ And I saw to the east another mountain higher than it, and between them a deep valley that had no breadth, and through it water was flowing beneath[a] the mountain. 4/ And to the west of this, another mountain lower than it and not rising very high, and a deep and dry valley beneath it, between them, and another deep and dry valley,[b] at the apex of the three mountains. 5/ And all the valleys were deep, of hard rock, and no tree was planted on them.

6   And I marveled at the mountain, and I marveled at the valley, I marveled exceedingly.

27:1   Then I said, "Why is this land blessed and all filled with trees, but this valley is cursed?"

2   Then <Sariel>[c] answered, one of the holy angels who was with me, and said to me, "This cursed valley is for those who are cursed forever. Here will be gathered all the cursed, who utter with their mouth an improper word against the Lord and speak hard things against his glory. Here they will be gathered, and here will be (their) habitation 3/ at the last times, in the days of righteous judgment in the presence of the righteous for all time. Here the godless[d] will bless the Lord of glory, the King of eternity. 4/ In the days of their judgment they will bless †in mercy†[e] in accordance with how he has apportioned to them."

5   Then I blessed the Lord of glory, and his glory I made known and praised magnificently.

---

a Eth *toward.*

b Aram evidently omitted *deep and dry.*

c Gk Eth read *Uriel.* Emendation follows 20:6, where Sariel's place in the sequence and his function agree with this vision. Aram at 9:1 indicates that the names are confused.

d Eth *the merciful,* perhaps influenced by *in mercy* in v 4.

e Meaning is obscure. Perhaps the text originally referred to a plea for mercy. Cf. 63:1, 5-6.

To the Paradise of Righteousness[a]

28:1   And from there I went to the midst of the mountain range
        of the desert. And I saw it desolate, and it alone was full
        of trees <and plants>. 2/ Water was pouring forth from
        above. 3/ Flowing like a copious watercourse, approximately
        to the northwest, it brought water and also dew from all
        around.

29:1   From there I went to another place in the desert, and I departed
        to the east of this mountain range. 2/ I saw trees <of the
        field> breathing fragrances of frankincense and myrrh, and
        their trees were like nut trees.

30:1   Beyond these I departed far to the east. And I saw another
        vast place—valleys of water, 2/ in which were aromatic cane
        like reeds. 3/ On the banks of these valleys I saw the fragrant
        cinnamon.

31:1   Beyond these valleys, I departed to the east. And I saw other
        mountains, and also on them I saw trees, from which flowed
        the nectar called storax and galbanum.

2   Beyond these mountains I was shown another mountain, and
        on it were aloe trees. All the trees were full of . . . . , and
        it was like the bark of the almond tree. 3/ When they grind
        this bark, it is sweeter than any perfume.

32:1   Beyond these mountains, approximately to their northeastern
        side I saw other mountains, filled with choice nard and *tspr*
        and cardamom and pepper.

2   From there I proceeded to the east of all these mountains, far
        from them to the east of the earth. And I passed over the Red
        Sea and departed far from it. And I crossed over the darkness,
        far from it.

3   I passed by the paradise of righteousness, and I saw from afar
        trees more plentiful and larger than these trees, differing

---

a The textual situation in these chapters is especially complex due to the pleth-
ora of sometimes obscure proper names, the technical nature of the subject matter,
and the disagreements among Gk, Eth, and two Aram mss. For details, see *1 Enoch 1*,
320–28.

from those—very large <and> beautiful and glorious and magnificent—and the tree of wisdom, whose fruit the holy ones eat and learn great wisdom. 4/ That tree is in height like the fir, and its leaves, like (those of) the carob, and its fruit like the clusters of the vine—very cheerful; and its fragrance penetrates far beyond the tree.

5   Then I said, "How beautiful is the tree and how pleasing in appearance."

6   Then <Gabriel>,[a] the holy angel who was with me, answered, "This is the tree of wisdom from which your father of old and your mother of old, who were before you, ate and learned wisdom. And their eyes were opened, and they knew that they were naked, and they were driven from the garden."

To the Ends of the Earth

33:1   And from there I proceeded to the ends of the earth, and I saw there great beasts, and they differed each from the other; and birds also, differing (in) their appearance and their beauty and their voices, differed each from the other.

To the east of these beasts I saw the ends of the earth, on which the heaven rests, and the gates of heaven open. 2/ I saw how the stars of heaven come forth, and I counted the gates from which they emerge, 3/ and I wrote down all their outlets, one by one, according to their number and their names, according to their conjunction and their position and their time and their months, as Uriel, the holy angel[b] who was with me, showed me. 4/ He showed me and wrote down for me everything, and also he wrote down their names and their appointed times and their functions.

---

a Raphael in Gk and Eth is emended to *Gabriel,* following the sequence in 20:7, and the consonance of Gabriel's responsibility there with the present station of Enoch's journey.

b For angel, Aram has [*one of the*] *watchers.* Cf. 22:6, note b.

Enoch's Journeys North, West, South, and East: A Summary

34:1   And from there I proceeded to the north, at the ends of the earth, and there I saw great and glorious wonders at the ends of the whole earth. 2/ There I saw three gates of heaven open in heaven. From them the winds in the north emerge. When they blow, (there is) cold and hail and hoarfrost and snow and dew and rain. 3/ Through one gate they blow for good, and when they blow through two of the gates, they blow with violence, and there is affliction on the earth.

35:1   From there I proceeded toward the west, at the ends of the earth, and I saw there three gates of heaven open, as I saw in the east, the same number of gates and the same number of outlets.

36:1   From there I proceeded toward the south, at the ends of the earth, and there I saw three gates of heaven open, and from there the south wind and dew and rain emerge.

2   From there I proceeded toward the east, at the ends of the earth, and there I saw three gates of heaven open toward the east and above them, small gates. 3/ Through each of these small gates pass the stars of heaven, and they proceed westward on the path that is shown them.

4   And when I saw, I blessed—and I shall always bless—the Lord of glory, who has wrought great and glorious wonders, to show his great deeds to his angels and to the spirits of human beings,[a] so that they might see the work of his might and glorify the deeds of his hands and bless him forever.

---

a All Eth mss add here *so that they might glorify his work and all his deeds,* which appears to be a doublet of the following two clauses whose parallelism seems original.

The Book of Parables

(Chapters 37–71)

Superscription and Introduction (Chapter 37)

37:1 ^aTHE VISION OF WISDOM THAT ENOCH SAW—the son of Jared,
the son of Mahalalel, the son of Kenan, the son of Enosh, the
son of Seth, the son of Adam.

2 This is the beginning of the words of wisdom,
> which I took up to recount to those who dwell on the
> earth.^b

Listen, O ancients, and look, you who come after—
> the words of the Holy One,^c which I speak in the presence
> of the Lord of Spirits.

3 It is profitable to speak these things at first,
> and from those who come after, let us not withhold the
> beginning of wisdom.

4 Until now there had not been given from the presence of the
> Lord of Spirits
> such wisdom as I have received according to my insight,

according to the good pleasure of the Lord of Spirits,
> by whom the lot of everlasting life was given to me.

5 Three parables were (imparted) to me,
> and I took (them) up and spoke to those who dwell on the
> earth.

---

a All Eth mss begin with *The second vision that he saw*, almost certainly a gloss that
postdates the section's incorporation into the corpus and relates the Parables to Enoch's
vision recounted in the Book of the Watchers.

b Eth *yabs*, lit. (*dry*) *land*. The Parables appear to use this noun and *medr* (*earth*)
synonymously and both are translated here as *earth*, unless a contrast is explicit with
the sea or water or with heaven.

c Many mss read *the holy words*.

The First Parable (Chapters 38–44)

The Coming Judgment of the Wicked

38:1   The First Parable.
        When the congregation of the righteous appears,
            the sinners are judged for their sins,
            and from the face of the earth they are driven;
2   And when the Righteous One[a] appears in the presence of the
            righteous,
            whose chosen works depend on the Lord of Spirits,
            and light appears to the righteous and chosen who dwell
                on the earth;
        Where (will be) the dwelling place of the sinners,
            and where (will be) the resting place of those who have
                denied the Lord of Spirits?
        It would have been better for them, if they had not been
            born.

3   When his hidden things are revealed to the righteous,
            the sinners will be judged,
            and the wicked will be driven from the presence of the
                righteous and chosen.
4   And thereafter, it will not be the mighty and exalted who
            possess the land,[b]
            and they will not be able to look at the face of the holy,
            for the light of the Lord of Spirits will have appeared on
                the face of the holy, righteous, and chosen.
5   And then the kings and mighty will perish,
            and they will be given into the hand of the righteous and
                holy,
6   and from then on, no one will seek mercy for them from the
            Lord of Spirits,
            for their life will be at an end.

---

a Some mss read *righteousness.*
b That is, the land of Israel, or an individual's land. Alternatively "the earth."

The Descent of the Angels

39:1   In those days, sons of the chosen and holy were descending
             from the highest heaven,
          and their seed was becoming one with the sons of men.
2   In those days Enoch received books of jealous wrath and rage
          and books of trepidation and consternation.[a]

Enoch's Ascent to Heaven

3   And in those days[b] a whirlwind snatched me up from the
             face of the earth
          and set me down within the confines of the heavens.

The Dwellings of the Righteous

4   And there I saw another vision—the dwellings of the holy
             ones,
          and the resting places of the righteous.
5   There my eyes saw their dwellings with his righteous angels
          and their resting places with the holy ones.
          And they were petitioning and interceding
             and were praying for the sons of men.
          And righteousness was flowing like water before them,
             and mercy like dew upon the earth;
             thus it is among them forever and ever.

The Dwelling of the Chosen One

6   And in that place[c] my eyes saw the Chosen One[d] of
             righteousness and faith,
          and righteousness will be his days,
          and the righteous and chosen will be without number
             before him forever and ever.

---

a All mss add what appears to be a misplaced variant of 38:6a.
b Some mss add *clouds and*; cf. 14:8.
c Some mss read *And in those days*.
d Some mss read *the place of the chosen*.

7 And I saw his dwelling[a] beneath the wings of the Lord of
   Spirits,
  and all the righteous and chosen were mighty before him
   like fiery lights.
 And their mouths were full of blessing,
  and their lips praised the name of the Lord of Spirits.
 And righteousness did not fail before him,
  nor did truth fail before him.[b]

8 There I wished to dwell,
  and my spirit longed for that dwelling.
 There my lot had been before,
  for thus it has been established concerning me in the
   presence of the Lord of Spirits.

Enoch Praises God

9 In those days I praised and exalted the name of the Lord of
   Spirits with blessing and praise,
  for he has established me for blessing and praise according
   to the good pleasure of the Lord of Spirits.

10 And for a long time, my eyes looked at that place,
  and I blessed him and praised him, saying,
 "Blessed is he, and may he be blessed from the beginning and
   forever."

11 In his presence there is no limit;
 He knew before the age was created what would be forever,
  and for all the generations that will be.

The Watchers Praise God

12 Those who sleep not bless you,
  and they stand in the presence of your glory;

---

a Some mss read *their dwellings*. See previous note.

b Line could be a doublet of the previous one, with a translation variant of Aram *qushtaʾ*. Verbs in this verse are translated as imperfects, but could be construed as future.

And they bless and praise and exalt, saying,
> "Holy, holy, holy is the Lord of Spirits,
> he fills the earth with spirits."

13 And there my eyes saw all who sleep not;
> they stand in his presence,
and they bless and say,
> "Blessed are you, and blessed is the name of the Lord
> forever and ever."

14 And my face was changed,
> for[a] I was unable to see.

The Four Archangels

40:1 And after this I saw thousands of thousands
> and ten thousand times ten thousand
> —they were innumerable and incalculable—
> who were standing in the presence of the glory of the Lord
> of Spirits.

2 I looked, and on the four sides of the Lord of Spirits, I saw four
figures different from those who sleep not. And I learned their
names, because the angel who went with me and showed me
all the hidden things made their names known to me.

3 And I heard the voices of those four figures
> uttering praise in the presence of the Lord of Glory.

4 The first voice blesses the Lord of Spirits forever and ever.

5 And the second voice I heard blessing the Chosen One
> and the chosen ones who depend on the Lord of Spirits.

6 And the third voice I heard petitioning and praying for those
> who dwell on the earth,
> and interceding in the name of the Lord of Spirits.

7 And the fourth voice I heard driving away the satans,
> and he did not let them come before the Lord of Spirits,
> to accuse those who dwell on the earth.

---

a Many mss read *until.*

8   And after that I asked the angel of peace who went with me
        and showed me everything that is hidden, "Who are these
        four figures that I have seen and whose words I have heard
        and written down?"

9   And he said to me,
        "The first one, <who>ᵃ is merciful and long-suffering, (is)
        Michael.
        The second one, who (is) in charge of every sickness and every
        wound of the sons of men, is Raphael.
        The third one, who (is) in charge of every power, is Gabriel.
        The fourth one, who (is) in charge of the repentance to hope
        of those who inherit everlasting life, his name (is) Phanuel."

10   These are the four angels of the Lord of Spirits;
            and the four voices I heard in those days.

The Judgment: An Anticipation

41:1   And after this, I saw all the secrets of heaven,
            how the kingdom is divided,
            and how human deeds are weighed in the balance.

2   There I saw the dwelling places of the chosen
            and the dwelling places of the holy ones.
        And my eyes saw there all the sinners who deny the name of
            the Lord of Spirits being driven away from there,
            and they dragged them off and they could not remain
                because of the scourge that went forth from the Lord of
                Spirits.ᵇ

9   For no angel hinders and no power is able to hinder,
            for the Judge sees them all and judges them all in his
                presence.

---

a Supplied by analogy with the structure of the next three sentences.

b As the mss stand, both 41:3-8 and 41:9 are separated from the sections to which
they are related. The rearrangement here seeks to remedy what appears to be a displace-
ment. See *1 Enoch 2*, 135.

The Descent of Wisdom and Iniquity

42:1   Wisdom did not find a place where she might dwell,
                 so her dwelling was in the heavens.
2   Wisdom went forth to dwell among the sons of men,
                 but she did not find a dwelling.
             Wisdom returned to her place,
                 and sat down in the midst of the angels.

3   Iniquity went forth from her chambers,
                 those whom she did not seek she found,
             and she dwelt among them
                 like rain in a desert
                 and dew in a thirsty land.

Astronomical Secrets

41:3   And there my eyes saw the secrets of the lightnings and the
                 thunder,
                 and the secrets of the winds, how they are divided to blow
                     upon the earth,
                 and the secrets of the clouds and the dew.
             And there I saw whence they proceed in that place,
                 and from there they saturate the dust of the earth.
4   There I saw closed storehouses, and from them the winds are
                 distributed;
                 the storehouse of the hail and the winds, the storehouse of
                     the mist and of the clouds,
                 and its cloud abides over the earth since the beginning of
                     the age.

5   And I saw the storehouses of the sun and the moon,
                 from which they emerge and to which they return, and
                     their glorious return,
                 and how the one is more praiseworthy than the other, and
                     their splendid course.

And they do not leave the course,
>and they neither extend nor diminish their course.
>And they keep faith with one another according to the
>oath that they have <sworn>.[a]

6 And first the sun emerges and completes[b] its path
>according to the command of the Lord of Spirits—
>and his name endures forever and ever.

7 And after that I saw[c] the invisible and visible path of the
>moon,
>>it completes the course of its path in that place by day and
>>by night.
>And the one is opposite the other[d] in the presence of the
>Lord of Spirits;
>>and they give praise and glory and do not rest,
>>for their praise is rest for them.

8 For the sun (makes) many revolutions for a blessing and a
>curse,
>>and the course of the path of the moon is light to the
>>righteous and darkness to the sinners,
>In the name of the Lord who distinguished[e] between light
>and darkness,
>>and divided the spirits of humanity,
>>and strengthened the spirits of the righteous in the name
>>of his righteousness.

43:1 And I saw other lightnings and stars of heaven;
>and I saw that he called them by their names,
>and they listened to him.

---

a Positing a corruption in Gk behind Eth, from *horkizein* to *oikizein* (*to dwell*,
Eth mss).

b Lit. *works, executes.*

c Verb appears in only two mss, but is necessary.

d Lit. *looks to.*

e Lit. *who created.*

2   I saw a righteous balance,
           how they are weighed according to their light,
           according to the breadth of their spaces
           and the day of their appearing.
        (I saw how) their revolution produces lightning,
           and their revolution is according to the number of the
              angels,
           and they keep their faith with one another.

3   And I asked the angel who went with me and showed me
           what was hidden, "What are these?"
4   And he said to me,
        "The Lord of Spirits has shown you a parable concerning
           them;
           these are the names of the holy ones who dwell on the
              earth
           and believe in the name of the Lord of Spirits forever and
              ever."

44:1   And another thing I saw regarding the lightning:
           how some stars arise and become lightning,
           and they cannot depart from their form.

The Second Parable (Chapters 45–57)

Introduction

45:1   This is the second parable concerning those who deny the
           name of the dwelling of the holy ones and of the Lord of
           Spirits.
2   To heaven they will not ascend, and on earth they will not
              come.
           Thus will be the lot of the sinners who have denied the
              name of the Lord of Spirits,
           who will be kept thus for the day of affliction and
              tribulation.

3   On that day, my Chosen One will sit on the throne of glory,
             and he will \<test\>[a] their works,
             and their dwelling place(s) will be innumerable.
         And their souls will be distressed within them,
             when they see my chosen ones,
             and those who appeal to my glorious name.

4   On that day, I shall make my Chosen One dwell among
             them[b],
             and I shall transform heaven and make it a blessing and a
             light forever;
5   and I shall transform the earth and make it a blessing.
         And my chosen ones I shall make to dwell on it,
             but those who commit sin and error will not set foot on it.
6   For I have seen and satisfied my righteous ones with peace
             and have made them to dwell in my presence.
         But the judgment of the sinners has drawn near to me,
             that I may destroy them from the face of the earth.

The Head of Days and the Son of Man

46:1   There I saw one who had a head of days,
             and his head was like white wool.[c]
         And with him was another, whose face was like the
             appearance of a man;
             and his face was full of graciousness like one of the holy
             angels.
2   And I asked the angel of peace,[d] who went with me and
             showed me all the hidden things, about that son of man

---

a Presuming a mistranslation of Aram *b⁽char*, which can mean *test* or *choose* (Eth mss). For another mistranslation in the next line, see *1 Enoch 2*, 150.

b Some mss read *I shall make him dwell among the chosen ones.*

c This verse reflects Dan 7:9, 13, with the term *ancient of days* being changed here- after to *Head of Days*. Term *son of man* refers to the human appearance of a divine figure and does not designate humanness.

d *Angel of peace*, the normal formulation in the Parables, occurs here in only one ms. Other mss read *one of the holy angels*, evidently a dittograph from the previous line.

—who he was and whence he was (and) why he went
with the Head of Days.

3   And he answered me and said to me,
"This is the son of man who has righteousness,
and righteousness dwells with him.
and all the treasuries of what is hidden he will reveal;
For the Lord of Spirits has chosen him,
and his lot has prevailed through truth
in the presence of the Lord of Spirits forever.

4   And this son of man whom you have seen—
he will raise the kings and the mighty from their couches,
and the strong from their thrones.
He will loosen the reins of the strong,
and he will crush the teeth of the sinners.

5   He will overturn the kings from their thrones and their
kingdoms,
because they do not exalt him or praise him,
or humbly acknowledge whence the kingdom was given to
them.

6   The face of the strong he will turn aside,
and he will fill them with shame.[a]
Darkness will be their dwelling,
and worms will be their couch.
And they will have no hope to rise from their couches,
because they do not exalt the name of the Lord of Spirits.

7   These are they who †judge† the stars of heaven,
and raise their hands against the Most High,
and tread upon the earth and dwell on it.
All their deeds manifest unrighteousness,
and their power (rests) upon their wealth.
Their faith is in the gods they have made with their hands,
and they deny the name of the Lord of Spirits.

8   And they persecute the houses of his congregation,
and the faithful who depend on the name of the Lord of
Spirits."

-----

a Some mss read *and shame will fill them.*

The Prayer of the Righteous and
the Intercession of the Holy Ones

47:1   In those days, there had arisen the prayer of the righteous,
        and the blood of the righteous one, from the earth into
           the presence of the Lord of Spirits. .

2   In these days the holy ones who dwell in the heights of
        heaven were uniting with one voice,

2c   and they were glorifying and praising and blessing the
        name of the Lord of Spirits,

2bd and were interceding and praying in behalf of the blood of
        the righteous that had been shed,
      and the prayer of the righteous, that it might not be in
        vain in the presence of the Lord of Spirits;
    that judgment might be executed for them,
      and endurance might not be their (lot) forever.

3   In those days I saw the Head of Days as he took his seat on
        the throne of his glory,
      and the books of the living were opened in his presence,
      and all his host, which was in the heights of heaven, and
        his court, were standing in his presence.

4   And the hearts of the holy ones were filled with joy,
      for the number of <the righteous>[a] was at hand;
      and the prayer of the righteous had been heard,
      and (a reckoning of) the blood of the righteous one had
        been required in the presence of the Lord of Spirits.

The Son of Man/Chosen One Is Named

48:1   In that place I saw the spring of righteousness, and it was
        inexhaustible,
    and many springs of wisdom surrounded it;
  And all the thirsty drank from them and were filled with
        wisdom;
    and their dwelling places were with the righteous and the
        holy and the chosen.

---

a Two mss read *the righteous one*, the others *righteousness*.

2   And in that hour that son of man was named in the presence
           of the Lord of Spirits,
         and his name, before the Head of Days.
3   Even before the sun and the constellations were created,
           before the stars of heaven were made,
           his name was named before the Lord of Spirits.

4   He will be a staff for the righteous,
           that they may lean on him and not fall;
         He will be the light of the nations,
           and he will be a hope for those who grieve in their hearts.
5   All who dwell on the earth will fall down and worship before
           him,
           and they will glorify and bless and sing hymns to the
           name of the Lord of Spirits.
6   For this (reason) he was chosen and hidden in his presence,
           before the world was created and forever.
7   And the wisdom of the Lord of Spirits has revealed him to
           the holy and the righteous;
           for he has preserved the lot of the righteous.
         For they have hated and despised this age of unrighteousness;
           Indeed, all its deeds and its ways they have hated in the
           name of the Lord of Spirits.
         For in his name they are saved,
           and he is the vindicator[a] of their lives.

8   In those days, downcast will be the faces of the kings of the
           earth,
           and the strong who possess the land, because of the deeds
           of their hands.
         For on the day of their tribulation and distress they will not
           save themselves;
9   and into the hand of my chosen ones I shall throw them.

---

a In other mss this is an abstract noun denoting God's good pleasure for their lives.

As straw in the fire and as lead in the water,
    thus they will burn before the face of the holy,
and they will sink before the face of the righteous;
    and no trace of them will be found.

10   And on the day of their distress there will be rest on the
        earth,
    and before them they will fall and not rise,
    and there will be no one to take them with his hand and
        raise them.
For they have denied the Lord of Spirits and his Anointed
    One.
Blessed be the name of the Lord of Spirits.

49:1   For wisdom has been poured out like water,
    and glory will not fail in his presence forever and ever.
2   For he is mighty in all the secrets of righteousness;
    and unrighteousness will vanish like a shadow,
    and will have no place to stand.
For the Chosen One has taken his stand in the presence of
    the Lord of Spirits;
    and his glory is forever and ever,
    and his might, to all generations.

3   And in him dwell the spirit of wisdom and the spirit of
        insight,
    and the spirit of instruction and might,
    and the spirit of those who have fallen asleep in
        righteousness.
4   And he will judge the things that are secret,
    and a lying word none will be able to speak in his
        presence;
For he is the Chosen One in the presence of the Lord of
    Spirits
    according to his good pleasure.

A Scenario for the End Time

The Glorification of the Holy and Chosen,
the Repentance of Others, and the Judgment
of the Unrepentant

50:1   In those days a change will occur for the holy and chosen,
           and the light of (many) days[a] will dwell upon them,
           and glory and honor will return to the holy.
2   On the day of distress, evil will be stored up[b] against the
              sinners,
           and the righteous will conquer in the name of the Lord of
              Spirits.

       And he will show (this) to the others,
           so that they repent and abandon the works of their hands.
3   And they will have honor[c] in the presence of[d] the Lord of
              Spirits,
           and in his name they will be saved;
       and the Lord of Spirits will have mercy on them,
           for great is his mercy.

4   But he is righteous in his judgment,
           and in the presence of his glory unrighteousness[e] will not
              stand;
       at his judgment the unrepentant will perish in his presence,
5   "And hereafter I will have no mercy on them," says the
              Lord of Spirits.

---

a Perhaps one should read *the light of day*. One ms reads *the ancient of days*.

b Exact wording of this clause varies in the mss.

c Most mss read *not have honor*, the easier and more suspicious reading.

d Some mss read *in the name of*, quite possibly a dittograph from v 2b or the next line.

e All but two mss read *and unrighteousness*, connecting the clause with the next line.

Resurrection, Judgment, Life on a Renewed Earth

51:1   In those days, the earth will give back what has been
        entrusted to it,
        and Sheol will give back what has been entrusted to it,[a]
        and destruction will restore what it owes.

5a   For in those days, my Chosen One will arise[b]
2   and choose the righteous and holy from among them,
        for the day on which they will be saved has drawn near.
3   And the Chosen One, in those days, will sit upon my
        throne,[c]
        and all the secrets of wisdom will go forth from the
        counsel of his mouth,
        for the Lord of Spirits has given (them) to him and
        glorified him.

4   In those days the mountains will leap like rams,
       and the hills will skip like lambs satisfied with milk;
       and the faces of all the angels in heaven will be radiant
       with joy,
5b   and the earth will rejoice,
       and the righteous will dwell on it,
       and the chosen will go[d] upon it.

Enoch's Journeys and Visions

The Six Mountains

52:1   After those days, in that place where I had seen all the visions
       of what is hidden—for I had been carried off in a whirlwind,
       and they had taken me to the West—

---

    a Wording of these two lines varies in the mss.

    b The tristichal form of vv 1 and 3 and the lack of any subject for the verb in v 2a
justify the transposition of this line here.

    c Some mss read *his throne.*

    d Some mss read *go and walk.* One ms reads *walk.*

2   There my eyes saw all the hidden things of heaven that will
     take place: a mountain of iron, and a mountain of copper,
     and a mountain of silver, and a mountain of gold, and a
     mountain of soft metal, and a mountain of lead.

3   And I asked the angel who went with me, "What are these
     things that I have seen in secret?"

4   And he said to me, "All these things that you have seen will
     be for the authority of his Anointed One, so that he may be
     powerful and mighty on the earth."

5   And that angel of peace answered and said to me, "Wait a little
     while, and all the hidden things that surround[a] the Lord of
     Spirits will be revealed to you.

6   These mountains that your eyes saw—the mountain of iron,
     and the mountain of copper, and the mountain of silver, and
     the mountain of gold, and the mountain of soft metal, and
     the mountain of lead—
     All these will be before the Chosen One like wax before the
          fire,
          and like the water that comes down from above upon
               these mountains,
          and they will be weak before his feet.

7   And in those days none will save himself either by gold or
          silver,
          and none will be able to flee.

8   And there will not be iron for war,
          nor a garment for a breastplate;
     copper will be of no use,
          and tin will be reckoned as nothing,
          and lead will not be desired.

9   All these will be rejected and be destroyed from the face of
          the earth,
          when the Chosen One appears before the Lord of Spirits."

---

a Some mss read *that the Lord of Spirits has established.*

The Valley of Punishment for the Kings and the Mighty

53:1 There my eyes saw a deep valley, and its mouth was open,
    and all who dwell on the land and the sea and the islands
        will bring it gifts and presents and tribute,
    but that valley will not become full.

2 Their hands commit lawless deeds,
    and everything that (the righteous) labor over, the sinners
        lawlessly devour.
  And from the presence of the Lord of Spirits the sinners will
        perish,
    and from the face of his earth they will be taken,
    and they will perish forever and ever.[a]

3 For I saw all the angels of punishment dwelling (there)[b] and
  preparing all the instruments of Satan.

4 And I asked the angel of peace who went with me, "These
  instruments—for whom are they preparing them?"

5 And he said to me, "They are preparing these for the kings and
  the mighty of this earth, that they may perish thereby."

6 And after this, the Righteous and Chosen One will cause the
    house of his congregation to appear;
    from then on, they will not be hindered in the name of
      the Lord of Spirits.

7 And these mountains will be in the presence of his
    righteousness as <wax>[c]
  and the hills will be like a fountain of water,
  and the righteous will rest from the oppression of the
    sinners.

---

a Indicating annihilation. Most have the negative, indicating everlasting punishment.

b Many mss read *going*. The accepted reading emphasizes that they have come here to work.

c Mss read *will* (*not*) *be in the presence of his righteousness* (or *in his presence*) *as the earth*. By analogy with 52:6 and in light of the next line, *medr* (*earth*) is emended to *maʿāra gerā* (*wax*).

The Valley of the Rebel Angels' Punishment

54:1   And I looked and turned to another part of the earth, and
            I saw there a deep valley with burning fire. {2/ And they
            brought the kings and the mighty and threw them into that
            deep valley.}[a] 3/ And there my eyes saw them making their
            instruments, iron chains of immeasurable weight.
4   And I asked the angel of peace who went with me, "For whom
            are these chains being prepared?"
5   And he said to me, "These are being prepared for the host of
            Azazel, that they might take them and throw them into the
            abyss of complete judgment, and with jagged rocks they will
            cover their jaws, as the Lord of Spirits commanded.
6   And Michael and Raphael and Gabriel and Phanuel will take
            hold of them on that great day, and throw them on that day
            into the burning furnace, that the Lord of Spirits may take
            vengeance on them, for their unrighteousness in becoming
            servants of Satan, and leading astray those who dwell on the
            earth."

The Flood (An Interpolated Digression)

7   In those days the punishment of the Lord of Spirits will come
                forth,
                    and he will open all the chambers of the waters that are
                        above the heavens
                    and the fountains that are beneath the earth.
8   And all the waters will be joined with the waters—
                    (the water) that is above the heavens is male,
                    the water that is beneath the earth is female—
9   And they will obliterate all who dwell on the earth
                    and who dwell beneath the ends of heaven.

---

a Line has been displaced. The kings and mighty belong in the previous valley
(53:5), not in this one, which is designated for the fallen angels (54:5).

10   And when they have recognized their iniquities that they
            have done on the earth,
        then by these they will be destroyed.

55:1   And after that, the Head of Days repented and said, "In vain
            have I destroyed all who dwell on the earth."

2   And he swore by his great name, "Henceforth I shall not do
            so to all who dwell on the earth.
        And I will set a sign in heaven,
            and it will be (a pledge of) faithfulness between me and
                them forever,
            as long as heaven is above the earth,
            and this is in accordance with my ordinance."

The Punishment of the Angels (continued)

3   "When I have desired to take hold of them by the hand of the
        angels, on the day of tribulation and distress in the face of
        my punishment and wrath, I will make my punishment and
        wrath dwell upon them," says the Lord of Spirits.

4   "Mighty kings who dwell on the earth, you will have to wit-
        ness my Chosen One, how he will sit on the throne of glory
        and judge Azazel and all his associates and all his host in the
        name of the Lord of Spirits."

56:1   And I saw there hosts of angels of punishment going, and they
        were holding <chains> of iron and bronze.

2   And I asked the angel of peace who went with me, "To whom
        are these who are holding (the chains) going?"

3   And he said to me, "To their chosen and beloved ones, that
        they may be thrown into the chasm of the abyss of the valley.

4   Then that valley will be filled with their chosen and beloved
            ones,
            and the days of their life will be at an end,
            and the days of their leading astray will henceforth not be
                reckoned."

The Scenario of the End Time Continued

The Eschatological War

5   In those days, the angels will assemble themselves,
           and hurl themselves toward the East against the Parthians
               and Medes.
       They will stir up the kings, and a spirit of agitation will come
           upon them,
           and they will shake them off their thrones.
       They will break out like lions from their lairs,
           and like hungry wolves in the midst of their flocks.
6   They will go up and trample the land of my chosen ones,[a]
           and the land of my chosen ones will be before them like a
               threshing floor and a (beaten) path;
7   but the city of my righteous ones will be a hindrance to
               their horses.

       They will begin (to make) war among themselves,
           and their right hand will be strong against them(selves),
       a man will not acknowledge his brother,
           nor a son, his father or his mother.
       Until the number of corpses will be enough due to their
           slaughter,
           and their punishment will not be in vain.
8   In those days, Sheol will open its mouth,
           and they will sink into it.
       And their destruction will be at an end;
           Sheol will devour the sinners from the presence of the
               chosen.[b]

---

a Some mss read *their chosen ones* and *his chosen ones* in this line and the next.
b Mss vary in these two lines, but the sense is clear.

A Second Host Travels to Jerusalem

57:1   After that I saw another host of chariots and people riding in
            them,
                and they came upon the winds from the East and the West
                toward the South,
2   and the noise of the rumbling of their chariots was heard.[a]
            When this commotion took place,
                the holy ones took note from heaven,
                and the pillars of the earth were shaken from their bases.
            It was heard from one end of the heaven to the other[b] in one
                moment,
3   and they all fell down and worshiped the Lord of Spirits.
            This is the end of the second parable.

The Third Parable (Chapters 58-69)

Introduction

58:1   And I began to speak the third parable concerning the righ-
            teous and concerning the chosen.
2   Blessed are you, righteous and chosen,
                for glorious (will be) your lot.
3   The righteous will be in the light of the sun,
                and the chosen, in the light of everlasting life.
            The days of their life will have no end,
                and the days of the holy will be innumerable.
4   They will seek the light and find righteousness with the Lord
                of Spirits;
                (there will be) peace for the righteous in the name of the
                Eternal Lord.

---

a Some mss omit the verb, i.e., *there was the noise, etc.*

b Lit. *from the ends of heaven to (its end).* Other mss vary, referring also to the ends
of the earth.

5   And after this it will be said to the holy ones,
           that they should seek in heaven the secrets of
               righteousness, the lot of faith;
       for the sun has risen upon the earth,[a]
           and darkness has passed away.
6   There will be light that does not cease,
           and to a limit of days they will not come;
       for darkness will first have been destroyed,
           and light will endure before the Lord of Spirits.
           {The light of truth will endure forever before the Lord of
           Spirits.}

The Secrets of the Winds and Other Heavenly Phenomena

59:1   In those days, my eyes saw the secrets of the lightnings and
           the luminaries and their laws;
           they flash for a blessing or for a curse, as the Lord of
           Spirits wills.
2   And there I saw the secrets of the thunder,
           †and (how) when it crashes in the heights of heaven,
           its sound is heard <in> the dwelling places of the earth,
       he showed me the sound of the thunder for peace and
           blessing, or for a curse†[b]
       according to the word of the Lord of Spirits.
3   After that, all the secrets of the luminaries and the lightnings
           were shown to me,
           how they flash for blessing and for satisfaction.[c]

---

   a Most mss read *it has become bright as the sun upon the earth.*

   b These three lines are corrupt and commentators dispute how to resolve the problem.

   c Two lines look like a doublet of v 1. Two factors support moving 60:11-23 to a
position before 60:1-10. (1) The reference to the *two monsters* in v 24 presumes vv 7-10
immediately before vv 24-25. (2) Moving vv 11-23 forward before 60:1 juxtaposes
material about the lightnings and thunders with the other cosmological material.

60:11   And the other angel who went with me and showed me what
is hidden told me
what is first and last in heaven in the height, and beneath the
earth in the abyss,
and at the ends of heaven and on the foundation of
heaven,

12   and in the storehouses of the winds,
how the winds are divided and how they are weighed,
and how the †springs†(?) of the winds are (divided and)
numbered,
according to the power of the wind,
and the power of the light of the moon,
and according to the power of righteousness.
And the divisions of the stars, according to their names,
and (how) all the divisions are made.

13   And the thunders, according to the places where they fall,
and all the divisions that are made among the lightnings,
that they may flash,
and their host, that they may obey at once.

14   For to the thunder resting places were given, as it awaits its
voice,
and the thunder and the lightning are not separated.
And (although) they are not one,
by the wind the two of them go and are not separated.

15   For when the lightning flashes, the thunder utters its voice,
and the wind, at the right time, causes it to rest,
and divides equally between them.
For the storehouse of their times is (like) that of the sand;
and each of them is checked by a rein,
and is turned back by the power of the wind
and driven thus according to the many regions of the
earth.

16   The wind of the sea is masculine and strong,
and according to the power of its strength,
it draws it back with a rein;
and thus it is driven and scattered into all the mountains
of the earth.

17   The wind of the frost is its (own) angel,
          and the wind of the hail is a good angel.
18   The wind of the snow (God) has released because of its
              power;
          and the spirit in it is special;
          and what arises from it is like smoke,
          and its name (is) frost.
19   And the wind of the mist is not mingled with them in their
              storehouses,
          but has a special storehouse, because its course is glorious,
          both in light and in darkness,
          and in winter and in summer
          and in its storehouse is an angel. [a]
20   The wind of the dew, its dwelling (is) at the ends of the
              heaven,
          and it is connected with the storehouses of the rain,
          and its course (is) in winter and in summer,
          and its clouds and the clouds of the mist are associated,
          and the one gives to the other.
21   And when the wind of the rain moves from its storehouse,
              the angels come and open the storehouse, and bring it out,
          and when it is scattered on all the dry land,
              it is joined with the water that is on the dry land;
          and whenever it is joined with the water on the dry land,
              . . . . . [b]
22   For the waters are for those who dwell on the dry land,
          for (they are) nourishment for the dry land from the Most
              High who is in heaven;
          therefore there is a measure for the rain,
          and the angels are given charge of it.
23   All these things I saw toward the garden of the righteous.

---

a Mss differ in their wording of this strange line.

b A line appears to have dropped out here.

The Flood and the Final Judgment

60:1   In the year 500, in the seventh month, on the fourteenth
         of the month, in the life of <Noah>,[a] in that parable I saw
         how a mighty quaking made the heaven of heavens quake,
         and the host of the Most High and the angels—thousands
         of thousands and ten thousand times ten thousand—were
         greatly disturbed.

2   And the Head of Days was sitting on the throne of his glory,
             and the holy and righteous angels were standing around
                 him.

3   And great trembling took hold of me, and fear seized[b] me,
             and my loins were crushed, and my kidneys were
                 loosened,
             and I fell on my face.

4   And Michael sent another angel from among the holy ones,
             and he raised me up,
             and when he raised me up, my spirit returned.
         For I had not been able to endure the appearance of that
                 host,
             and its turmoil and the quaking of the heavens.

5   And Michael said to me,
         "What have you seen, that you are so disturbed?
             Until today has the day of his mercy lasted,
             and he has been merciful and long suffering to those who
                 dwell on the earth.

6   And when the day and the power and the punishment and
                 the judgment come, which the Lord of Spirits has
                 prepared
             for those who do not[c] worship the righteous <judge>,[d]
             and for those who deny the righteous judgment,
             and for those who take his name in vain . . .

---

a All mss read *Enoch*.

b Some good mss omit the verb, but cf. 14:13c-14 on which this is based.

c All but one ms omit the negative, which seems necessary, however.

d Emended from *judgment*, perhaps reflecting a mistranslation of Aram *dyn*. See
Knibb, *Enoch* 2:143.

And that day has been prepared
>for the elect, a covenant,
>for the sinners, a visitation."[a]

{7   And on that day two monsters were separated—the female monster whose name is Leviathan, to dwell in the depth of the sea, above the fountains of the waters.

8   But the name of the male is Behemoth, who occupies with his breast the trackless desert named †Dundayn†[b] east of the garden where the chosen and righteous dwell, where my great-grandfather was taken up, the seventh from Adam, the first man whom the Lord of Spirits created.

9   And I asked another angel[c] to show me the might of those monsters, how they were separated in one day and were thrown the one into the depth of the sea, and the other into the dry land of the desert.

10   And he said to me, "Here, son of man, you wish to know what is hidden."

24   And the angel of peace who was with me said, "These two monsters, prepared according to the greatness of the Lord, will provide food for <the chosen and righteous>}[d]
. . . . . so that the punishment of the Lord of Spirits rests upon them,
>in order that the punishment of the Lord of Spirits does not go forth in vain.

---

a The bracketed passage that follows interrupts the continuity of 60:6 and 60:24c and may be an interpolation in the text.

b One of several forms of the name, this one is similar to *Doudael* in 10:4.

c Or *the other angel*: Other mss read *this angel* and *that angel*.

d Text is defective and is followed by a section that appears to connect to v 6 above. Mss have a snarl of duplications and omissions in the next five lines. Text follows explanation of Knibb, *Enoch* 1:170.

And the children will be killed with their mothers,
and the children with their fathers.

25   When the punishment of the Lord of Spirits rests upon
them,
afterwards will be the judgment according to his mercy
and his longsuffering."

The Angels Prepare to Gather the Righteous

61:1   And I saw in those days, long cords were given to those angels,
and they took for themselves wings and flew and went toward
the North.
2   And I asked the angel, "Why did these take the cords and go?"
And he said to me, "They went so that they may measure."
3   And the angel who went with me said to me,
"These will bring the measurements of the righteous,
and the ropes of the righteous to the righteous;
so that they may rely on the name of the Lord of Spirits
forever and ever.
4   And the chosen will begin to dwell with the chosen;
and these are the measurements that will be given to faith,
and they will strengthen righteousness.

5   And these measurements will reveal all the secrets of the
depths of the earth,
and those who were destroyed by the desert,
and those who were devoured by beasts,
and those who were devoured by the fish of the sea;
so that they may return and rely on the day of the Chosen
One,
for no one will be destroyed in the presence of the Lord of
Spirits,
and no one is able to be destroyed."

The Enthronement of the Chosen One

61:6   And all who are in the heights of heaven received a command,
             and power and one voice and one light like fire were given
             to him.^a

7   And that one, before anything, they blessed with (their) voice,
             and they exalted and glorified with wisdom;
          and they were wise in speech and in the spirit of life.

8   And the Lord of Spirits seated the Chosen One upon the
             throne of glory;
          and he will judge all the works of the holy ones in the
             heights of heaven,
          and in the balance he will weigh their deeds.

9   And when he will lift up his face
          to judge their secret ways according to the word of the
             name of the Lord of Spirits,
          and their paths according to the way of the righteous
             judgment of the Lord of Spirits,
       they will all speak with one voice,
          and bless and glorify and exalt
          and sanctify the name of the Lord of Spirits.

10   And all the host of the heavens will cry out and all the holy
             ones in the heights,
          and the host of the Lord—the Cherubin, the Seraphin,
             and the Ophannin,
       and all the angels of power and all the angels of the
             dominions,
          and the Chosen One and the other host who are on the
             dry land and over the water on that day.

11   And they will raise one voice,
          and they will bless and glorify and exalt
       with the spirit of faithfulness and with the spirit of wisdom,
          and with (a spirit of)^b long suffering and with the spirit of
             mercy,

---

a A few mss add *was given to them*, which fills out the parallelism.

b Phrase appears in only a few mss, but is implied.

and with the spirit of judgment and peace and with the
   spirit of goodness.
And they will all say with one voice,
"Blessed (is he), and blessed be the name of the Lord of Spirits forever and ever."
12   And all who sleep not in the heights of heaven will bless him,
         and all the holy ones who are in heaven will bless him,
         and all the chosen who dwell in the garden of life.
      And every spirit of light that is able to bless and glorify and
         exalt and sanctify your blessed name,
         and all flesh that in excess of (its) power glorifies and
            blesses your name forever and ever.
13   For great is the mercy of the Lord of Spirits,
         and he is slow to anger;
      and all his deeds and all his mighty acts, as many as he has
         done,
         he has revealed to the righteous and the chosen in the
            name of the Lord of Spirits.

The Chosen One Presides Over the Great Judgment

The Confrontation

62:1   And thus the Lord commanded the kings and the mighty and
          the exalted and those who possess the land,[a] and he said,
       "Open your eyes and lift up your horns,
          if you are able to recognize the Chosen One."
2   And the Lord of Spirits <seated him>[b] upon the throne of his
          glory,
          and the spirit of righteousness was poured upon him.
       And the word of his mouth will slay all the sinners,
          and all the unrighteous will perish from his presence.

---

a Two mss: others read *who inhabit* (or *dwell on*) *the earth.*

b Emending *wanabara* (*he sat*) to *waʾanbaro,* or positing a mistranslation of Aram.
Cf. 62:5, as well as 51:3; 55:4; 61:8; 69:29. The spirit of righteousness is not poured
out on God (next line).

3   And there will stand up on that day all the kings and the
          mighty
      and the exalted and those who possess the land.
      And they will see and recognize that he sits on the throne of
          his glory;
      and righteousness is judged in his presence,
      and no lying word is spoken in his presence.
4   And pain will come upon them as (upon) a woman in labor,[a]
          when the child enters the mouth of the womb,
      and she has difficulty in giving birth.
5   And one group of them will look at the other;
      and they will be terrified and will cast down their faces,
          and pain will seize them when they see that Son of Man
              sitting on the throne of his glory.
6   And the kings and the mighty and all who possess the land
          will bless and glorify and exalt him who rules over all, who
              was hidden.

7   For from the beginning the Son of Man was hidden,
          and the Most High preserved him in the presence of his
              might,
      and he revealed him to the chosen.
8   And the congregation of the chosen and holy will be sown;
      and all the chosen will stand in his presence on that day.

      The Condemnation of the Kings and the Mighty

9   And all the kings and the mighty and the exalted and those
          who rule the land will fall on their faces in his
              presence;
      and they will worship and set their hope on that Son of
          Man,
      and they will supplicate and petition for mercy from
          him.

---

a All mss add *for whom birth is difficult*, almost certainly a double reading for v 4c.

10   But the Lord of Spirits himself will press them,
            so that they will hasten to depart from his presence;
        and their faces will be filled with shame,
            and the darkness will grow deeper on their faces.
11   And he will deliver them[a] to the angels for punishment,
            so that they may exact retribution from them
            for the iniquity that they did to his children and his
                chosen ones.
12   And they will be a spectacle for the righteous and for his
                chosen ones;
            and they will rejoice over them,
        because the wrath of the Lord of Spirits rests upon them,
            and his sword is drunk with them.

The Salvation of the Righteous and Chosen

13   And the righteous and the chosen will be saved on that day;
            and the faces of the sinners and the unrighteous they will
                henceforth not see.
14   And the Lord of Spirits will abide over them,
            and with that Son of Man they will eat,
            and they will lie down and rise up forever and ever.

15   And the righteous and chosen will have arisen from the earth,
            and have ceased to cast down their faces,
            and have put on the garment of glory.
16   And this will be your garment, the garment of life from the
                Lord of Spirits;
            and your garments will not wear out,
            and your glory will not fade in the presence of the Lord of
                Spirits.

---

a Mss read variously *and he delivered them, and they will deliver* (or *take*) *them.*

The Confession of the Kings and the Mighty

63:1   In those days, the mighty and the kings who possess the land
        will implore the angels of his punishment, to whom
        they have been delivered,
    to give them a little respite
that they might fall down and worship in the presence of the
        Lord of Spirits,
    and that they might confess their sins in his presence.

2   They will bless and glorify the Lord of Spirits and say,
"Blessed is the Lord of Spirits and the Lord of kings,
    and the Lord of the mighty and the Lord of the rich,
    and the Lord of glory and the Lord of wisdom.

3   Your power is splendid in every secret thing for all
        generations,
    and your glory, forever and ever.
Deep are all your secrets and without number,
    and your righteousness is beyond reckoning.

4   Now we know that we should glorify and bless the Lord of
        the kings,
    and him who reigns over all kings."

5   And they will say,
"Would that we might be given respite,
    that we might glorify and praise
    and make confession in the presence of your glory.

6   Now we desire a little respite and do not find it,
    we pursue it and do not lay hold of it.
And light has vanished from our presence,
    and darkness is our dwelling forever and ever.

7   For in his presence we did not make confession,
    nor did we glorify the name of the Lord of the kings;
Our hope was on the scepter of our kingdom
    and <throne of>[a] our glory.

---

a Mss vary. Emendation brings over *throne* from the previous line in some mss to create parallelism in the cliche *throne of glory*.

8   But on the day of our affliction and tribulation it does not
          save us,
          nor do we find respite to make confession,
     that our Lord is faithful in all his deeds and his judgment
          and his justice,
          and his judgments have no respect for persons.
9   And we vanish from his presence because of our deeds,
          and all our sins are reckoned in righteousness."

10   Now they will say to themselves,
     "Our lives[a] are full of ill-gotten wealth,
          but it does not prevent us from descending into the flame
          of the torment of Sheol."
11   And after that their faces will be filled with darkness and
          shame in the presence of that Son of Man;
          and from his presence they will be driven,
          and a sword will abide before him in their midst.
12   Thus says the Lord of Spirits,
     "This is the law and the judgment of the mighty and the
          kings
          and the exalted and those who possess the land
          in the presence of the Lord of Spirits."

Enoch Sees the Fallen Angels

64:1   And other figures I saw hidden in that place.
2   I heard the voice of the angel saying, "These are the angels
       who descended upon the earth. And what was hidden they
       revealed to human beings, and they led human beings astray
       so that they committed sin."

---

a Lit. *our souls*, or perhaps pleonastically *we*.

Some Noachic Fragments[a]

Noah's Visions of the Earth's Destruction and Enoch's Interpretation

65:1   In those days Noah saw that the earth had tilted and its destruction was near. 2/ And he set out from there and went to the ends of the earth and cried to his great-grandfather, Enoch. And Noah said three times with a bitter voice, "Hear me, hear me, hear me."[b] 4/ And after that there was great quaking upon the earth, and a voice was heard from heaven, and I fell on my face. 5/ And Enoch my great-grandfather came and stood by me and said to me, "Why have you cried to me with bitter cry and lamentation?" 3/ I said to him, "Tell me what is happening upon the earth, that the earth staggers so and shakes, lest I perish with it."[c]

9   And after this, my great-grandfather Enoch took me by my hand and raised me up and said to me, "Go, for I have asked the Lord of Spirits about the quaking upon the earth.

6   "A command has gone forth from the presence of the Lord against the inhabitants of the earth, that their end is accomplished, for they have learned all the secrets of the angels and all the violence of the satans, and all their powers, the hidden secrets and all the powers of those who practice sorcery, and the powers of (brightly) color(ed garments), and the powers of those who cast molten (images) for all the earth. 7/ And how silver is produced from the dust of the earth and how soft metal <is poured out>[d] on the earth. 8/ For lead and tin are not produced from the earth like the former; there is a fountain that produces them, and an angel stands in it, and the angel is preeminent."

———

a The section 65:1—69:1 contains traditions associated more with Noah than Enoch. Their relationship to one another and to the Book of Parables is difficult to ascertain.

b V 3 is transposed after vv 4-5 because it presupposes the content of vv 4-5.

c V 9 is transposed here because Enoch, not Noah (v 3), is the speaker in vv 6-8, and v 10 presupposes the rebel angels as the antecedent to *their* and *they* immediately before it.

d Emending *yekawwen* (*exists*) to *yetkaᶜᶜaw*, in keeping with the explanation in v 8.

10   And he said to me,
            "Because of their iniquity, their judgment has been
                    accomplished and will not be withheld[a] in my
                    presence;
                because of the sorceries[b] that they have searched out and
                    learned,
                the earth will be destroyed, and those who dwell on it.
11   And these will never have a place of refuge forever,[c]
                for they have shown them what is hidden, and they are
                    judged.
            But as for you, my son, the Lord of Spirits knows that you
                    are pure and blameless of this reproach concerning the
                    mysteries.
12   And he has established your name among the holy ones,
                and he will preserve you from among those who dwell on
                    the earth,
            And he has established your righteous seed[d] (to be) kings and
                    for great honors.
                And from your seed there will flow a fountain of the
                    righteous and the holy,
                and they will be without number forever."

66:1   And after this, he showed me the angels of punishment, who
                are ready to go forth and let loose all the power of the water
                that is beneath the earth, that it might be for the judgment
                and destruction of all who reside and dwell on the earth.
2   And the Lord of Spirits commanded the angels who were
                    going forth,
                that they not raise their hands, but that they keep watch;
                for these angels were in charge of the power of the waters.
3   And I went forth from the presence of Enoch.

---

a Positing a corruption from Aram *cḥ'shak* to *cḥ'shab* (*reckon*, all Eth mss).

b Positing a corruption from Aram *chrshy'* to *chdshy'* (*months*, all Eth mss). See
Charles, *Enoch*, 131; Knibb, *Enoch* 2:155.

c Or (*possibility of*) *repentance*.

d Lit. *seed*, that is, descendants.

The Divine Oracle about the Flood

67:1   And in those days the word of God came to me and said to
            me,
        "Noah, your lot has come up to me,
            a lot without blame, a lot of love and uprightness.
2   And now the angels are making a wooden (vessel),
            and when the angels have completed that task,
            I will put my hand upon it and protect it.
        And from it will come the seed of life,
            and a change will take place,
            so that the earth will not remain desolate.
3   And I will establish your seed in my presence forever and
            ever,
            and I will scatter those who dwell with you,
        and I will not (again) bring temptation on the face of the
            earth,**a**
            and they will be blessed and be multiplied on the earth, in
            the name of the Lord."

A Vision of Punishment

4   And he will confine those angels who showed iniquity in that
        burning valley that my great-grandfather Enoch had shown
        me previously in the West by the mountains of gold and sil-
        ver and iron and soft metal and tin.
5   And I saw that valley in which there was a great disturbance
        and troubling of the waters. 6/ And when all this happened,
        from that fiery molten metal and the troubling of (the
        waters) in that place, the smell of sulfur was generated, and it
        mixed with those waters; and the valley of those angels who
        had led (humans) astray burned beneath that ground. 7/ And
        through the valleys of that (area) rivers of fire issue, where
        those angels will be judged who led astray those who dwell
        on the earth.

---

    a Here and throughout this section the author employs the noun *yabs* (lit. [*dry*]
land).

8   And in those days those waters (will serve) the kings and the mighty and the exalted and those who dwell on the earth, for the healing of (their) flesh[a] and the judgment of their spirits. And their spirits are full of pleasure, so that their flesh will be judged, because they denied the Lord of Spirits. And they see their judgment every day and do not believe in his name. 9/ And the more their flesh is burnt, the more a change takes place in their spirits, forever and ever, because before the Lord of Spirits no one speaks a lying word. 10/ For judgment will come upon them because they believe in the pleasure of their flesh, but they deny the Lord of Spirits.

11   And those same waters will be changed in those days, for when those angels are judged in those waters, those springs of water will change their temperature, and when the angels come up, the waters of those springs will be changed and become cold.

12   And I heard Michael answer and say, "This judgment with which the angels are judged is a testimony for the kings and the mighty who possess the land. 13/ For these waters of judgment (serve) for the healing of the flesh of the kings,[b] and for the pleasure of their flesh, and they do not see and do not believe that those waters will be changed and become a fire that burns forever."[c]

{68:1   And after this, my great-grandfather gave me the explanation of all the secrets in a book, and the parables that were given to him, and gathered them for me in the words of the Book of Parables.}

A Fragment of a Conversation between Michael and Raphael

2   And on that day, Michael answered and said to Raphael, "The power of the spirit seizes me and aggravates me, because of the harshness of the judgment of the secrets, the judgment

---

a Many mss read *their soul and body.*

b Positing a corruption of Aram *mlkʾ* (*kings*) to *mlʾkʾ* (*angels*, in all Eth mss).

c The next verse presupposes the existence of the book of which it is a part and appears to be an interpolation.

of the angels;[a] for who can endure the harshness of the judgment that has been executed before which they melt?"

3   And again Michael answered and said to Raphael, "Who is
there who would not soften his heart[b] over it, and whose
kidneys would not be troubled by this word? Judgment[c] has
gone forth against them, who have led them out thus."

4   But when they stood before the Lord of Spirits, Michael
spoke thus to Raphael, "I will not take their part under
the eye of the Lord, because the Lord of Spirits is angry
with them, because they act as if they were like the Lord.
5/ Therefore, everything that is hidden will come upon them
forever and ever; for no angel or human will receive their lot,
but they alone have received their judgment forever and ever.
69:1/ And after this judgment, they will trouble them and
aggravate them, because they have shown this to those who
dwell on the earth."

Two Lists of the Fallen Angels[d]

69:2   Look, the names of those angels, {and these are their names:
their first is Shemihazah; and the second is Arteqoph; the
third is <Remashel>; the fourth is Kokabel; the fifth is
†Turel†; the sixth is Ramel; the seventh is Daniel; the eighth
is Ziqel; the ninth is Baraqel; the tenth is Asael; the eleventh is Hermani; the twelfth is Matarel; the thirteenth is
†Basasel†; the fourteenth is Ananel; the fifteenth is †Turel†;
the sixteenth is Shamsiel; the seventeenth is <Saḥriel> ; the
eighteenth is <Tummiel>; the nineteenth is <Turiel>; the

---

a   Some mss omit *of the angels.*

b   The oldest mss read *whose heart does not become guilty.*

c   Some mss, connecting this word with the previous one, read *word of judgment.*

d   The two lists here (vv 2-3; 4-12) correspond to the double list in 6:7; 8:1-3, one a
simple list, the other explicating the functions of some angels. The first list corresponds
to 6:7, except that the thirteenth name has no counterpart and the following names are
pushed back one position, resulting in twenty-one rather than twenty names. Where
possible, corruptions in the names are emended to match 6:7. Others are left as they
are in the Eth.

twentieth is <Yamiel>; the twenty-first is †Azazel†. 3/ These are the chiefs of their angels and their names, and the leaders of their hundreds, and the leaders of their fifties, and the leaders of their tens.}

4   And the name of the first is Yeqon, this is the one who led all the children of the angels astray and brought them down upon the earth, and led them astray through the daughters of men.

5   And the name of the second is Asbe'el. This one gave evil counsel to the children of the holy angels, and led them astray so that they ruined their bodies through the daughters of men.

6   And the name of the third is Gadre'el. This is the one who showed all the blows of death to the sons of men, and he led Eve astray, and he showed[a] the shield and the coat of mail and the sword for battle and all the implements of death to the sons of men. 7/ And from his hand they have gone forth against those who dwell on the earth from that day and forever and ever.

8   And the name of the fourth is †Penemue†. This one showed the sons of men the bitter and the sweet and showed them all the secrets of their wisdom. 9/ He gave humans knowledge about writing with ink and papyrus, and therefore many went astray from of old and forever and until this day. 10/ For humans were not born for this purpose, to confirm their trustworthiness through pen and ink. 11/ For humans were not created to be different from the angels, so that they should remain pure and righteous. And death, which ruins everything, would not have laid its hand on them. But through this, their knowledge, they are perishing, and through this power it devours us.

12   And the name of the fifth is Kasdeya. This is the one who showed the sons of men all the evil blows of spirits and demons, and the blows of the foetus in the womb, so that it aborts, and {the blow of the soul,} the bite of the serpent,

---

a All mss add *the implements of death*, a dittograph of the last words of the Eth verse.

and the blow that comes in the noonday heat, the son of the serpent, whose name (is) Taba‘et.

The Angels and the Cosmic Oath

69:13   This is the number of Kasbe'el, the chief of the oath, which he showed to the holy ones when he was dwelling on high in glory, and its (*or* his) name (is) Beqa. 14/ This one told Michael that he should show him the secret name, so that they might mention it in the oath,[a] so that those who showed the sons of men everything that was in secret might quake at the name and the oath. 15/ And this is the power of this oath, for it is powerful and strong, and he placed this oath *aka*[b] in the hand of Michael. 16/ And these are the secrets of this oath, and they are strong through his oath.
         And <through that oath> the heaven was suspended . . .
         . . . .
         before the age was created and forever.[c]

17   Through it the earth[d] was founded upon the waters,
                 and from the hidden (recesses) of the mountains come
                     forth the beautiful waters,
                 from the creation of the age and forever.

18   And through that oath the sea was created,
                 and as its foundation, for the time of wrath, he placed for
                     it the sand,
                 and it does not pass over it from the creation of the age
                     and forever.

19   And through that oath the <pillars of the> deep were made
                     firm,
                 and they have stood and are not shaken from their place
                     from of old and forever.

---

    a Many mss have a longer and evidently dittographic reading of this sentence.

    b Corrupt: One ms reads ʾ*ekuy* (*evil* [*oath*]).

    c By consensus, the text of these two (three) lines is disturbed. Reconstruction presumes a tristiche analogous to those that follow.

    d Some mss read *through it also the earth* or *through it, and the earth*.

20   And through that oath the sun and the moon complete their
              course,
          and they do not transgress their commands from of old
              <and forever>.ᵃ
21   And through that oath the stars complete their courses,
              and he calls their names,
              and they answer him from of old and forever.
22   {And likewise the spirits of the water, of the winds, and all the
          breezes and their paths, from all the quarters of the winds.
          23/ And there are preserved the voices of the thunder and
          the light of the lightnings. And there are preserved the store-
          houses of the hail and the storehouses of the hoarfrost, and
          the storehouses of the mist and the storehouses of the rain
          and the dew. 24/ And all of these confess and give thanks
          before the Lord of Spirits, and they glorify (him) with all
          their might, and their food is in all thanksgiving, and they
          give thanks and glorify and exalt in the name of the Lord of
          Spirits forever and ever.}
25   And over them this oath is mighty,
              and by it they are preserved,
          {and their paths are preserved,}
              and their courses will not perish.

*The Judgment: A Concluding Summary*ᵇ

26   And they had great joy,
              and they blessed and glorified and exalted,
              because the name of that Son of Man had been revealed to
              them.

---

a Some mss omit this phrase, which is included here by analogy with the previous
units.

b This passage provides a conclusion to the scene in chapters 62–63, probably
indicating a long interpolation from 64:1—69:25.

27   And he sat on the throne of his glory,
            and the whole judgment was given to the Son of Man,
            and he will make sinners vanish and perish[a]from the face
                of the earth.
28   And those who led the world astray will be bound in chains,
            and in the assembly place of their destruction they will be
                shut up;
            and all their works will vanish from the face of the earth,

29   And from then on there will be nothing that is corruptible;
            for that Son of Man has appeared.
        And he has sat down on the throne of his glory,
            and all evil will vanish from his presence.
        And the word of that Son of Man will go forth
            and will prevail in the presence of the Lord of Spirits.

        This is the third parable of Enoch.

A Set of Concluding Appendices (Chapters 70–71)

Enoch Is Taken Away

70:1   And after this, while he was living, his name was lifted up
            into the presence of that Son of Man
        and into the presence of the Lord of Spirits
            from among those who dwell on the earth.
2   He was lifted up on the chariots of the wind,[b]
            and his name departed <from> among them.[c]

Enoch's Account of His Ascent

He Is Taken to the Garden of the Chosen and Righteous

3   And from that day, I was not reckoned among them; and
        he set me between two winds, between the North and the

---

a Among the various readings of the mss, this one alone makes sense.
b Or *the spirit.*
c Emending *among them* (a dittograph from the next line) to fit the verb *depart.*

West, where the angels took cords to measure for me the place of the chosen and the righteous. 4/ And there I saw the first fathers and the righteous, who were dwelling in that place from of old.

Enoch Ascends to Heaven and Sees the Heavenly Secrets

71:1 And after that, my spirit was taken away,
            and it ascended to heaven.
       And I saw the sons of the holy angels,
            and they were stepping on flames of fire;
       and their garments were white, as were their tunics,
            and the light of their faces was like snow.
2   And I saw two rivers of fire,
            and the light of that fire shone like hyacinth,
            and I fell on my face before the Lord of Spirits.
3   And the angel Michael, one of the archangels, took me by
                  my right hand and raised me up,
            and he brought me out to all the secrets;
       and he showed me all the secrets of mercy,
            and he showed me all the secrets of righteousness.
4   And he showed me all the secrets of the ends of heaven and
                  all the treasuries of the stars,
            and all the luminaries go forth from there before the holy
                  ones.

Enoch Ascends to the Heavenly Palace

5   And he took my spirit—even me, Enoch—to the heaven of
                  heavens,
       and I saw there,[a] as it were, <a house>[b] built of hailstones,
            and between those stones were tongues of living fire.

---

a Transposing *in that light* to v 6a, where it has a referent in the previous line.
b Emending *botu* (*in it*) to *bēta*, which is presupposed in v 6a.

6   And my spirit saw \<in that light\>[a] a circle that encircled that
          house of fire,
          from the four sides of that \<house\> (came) rivers full of
              living fire,
          and they encircled that house.
7   And around it (were) Seraphin and Cherubin, and
          Ophannin,
          and those who sleep not,
          but guard the throne of his glory.
8   And I saw angels that could not be counted,
          thousands of thousands and ten thousand times ten
              thousand;
          they were surrounding that house.
     And Michael and Raphael and Gabriel and Phanuel,
          and the holy angels who (are in) the heights of heaven,
          were going in and out in that house.

Enoch Sees the Angels and the Head of Days

9   And there came out of that house
          Michael and Raphael and Gabriel and Phanuel
          and many holy angels without number.
10   And with them was the Head of Days,
          and his head was white and pure as wool,
          and his garments were indescribable.
11   And I fell on my face,
          and all my flesh melted,
          and my spirit was transformed.
     And I cried out with a loud voice, with a spirit of power,
          and I blessed and praised and exalted.
12   And those blessings that went forth from my mouth
          were acceptable in the presence of that Head of Days.

---

a See note a.

Enoch Is Identified as the Son of Man

13   And that Head of Days came with Michael and Raphael and
          Gabriel and Phanuel,
         and thousands and tens of thousands of angels without
            number.

14   And he[a] came to me and greeted me with his voice and said
          to me,
        "You (are) that Son of Man who was born for righteousness,
          and righteousness dwells on you,
          and the righteousness of the Head of Days will not forsake
            you."

15   And he said to me,
        "He proclaims peace to you in the name of the age that is to
          be,
          for from there peace has proceeded from the creation of
            the age,
          and thus you will have it forever and forever and ever.

16   And all will walk on your path since righteousness will never
          forsake you;
          with you will be their dwelling and with you, their lot,
          and from you they will not be separated forever and
            forever and ever.

17   And thus there will be length of days with that Son of Man,
          and there will be peace for the righteous, and the path of
            truth for the righteous,
          in the name of the Lord of Spirits forever and ever."

---

a *wawe'etu mal'ak*: some mss read *and he* (*wawe'etu*). Does the Deity approach
Enoch and speak of himself in the third person? If not, who is "that angel." The text
mentions four angels

The Book of the Luminaries

(Chapters 72–82)

Introduction

72:1   THE BOOK ABOUT THE MOTION OF THE HEAVENLY LUMINARIES all as they are in their kinds, their jurisdiction, their time, their name, their origins, and their months which Uriel, the holy angel who was with me (and) who is their leader, showed me. The entire book about them, as it is, he showed me and how every year of the world will be forever, until a new creation lasting forever is made.

The Law of the Sun (72:2-37)

2   This is the first law of the luminaries: the luminary (called) the sun has its emergence through the heavenly gates in the east and its setting through the western gates of the sky. 3/ I saw six gates through which the sun emerges and six gates through which the sun sets. The moon rises and sets in those gates and the leaders of the stars with the ones they lead, six in the east and six in the west, all of them—one directly after the other. There are many windows on the right and left of those gates.

4   The first one to emerge is the great luminary whose name is the sun; its roundness is like the roundness of the sky. It is entirely filled with fire, which gives light and heat. 5/ The wind blows the chariot where it rises, and the sun sets from the sky and goes back through the north in order to reach the east. It is guided so that it enters that gate and gives light in the firmament. 6/ This is how it emerges in the first month

96

through the large gate; it emerges through that fourth one of those six gates on the side where the sun rises. 7/ In that fourth gate from which the sun emerges in the first month there are twelve open windows from which heat comes out when they are open at their times. 8/ When the sun rises in[a] the sky it emerges through that fourth gate for thirty mornings, and it accurately goes down in the fourth gate on the west side of the sky. 9/ During those days, day becomes longer than day and night becomes shorter than night for thirty days. 10/ On that day the daytime is two units[b] more than the night—one-ninth, with the daytime being exactly ten parts, and the night exactly eight parts. 11/ The sun emerges from that fourth gate and sets through the fourth (gate). It returns to the fifth gate in the east for thirty mornings, and it emerges from it and sets through the fifth gate. 12/ Then the daytime becomes longer by two (additional) parts: the daytime is eleven parts, while the night decreases and is seven parts. 13/ It returns to the east and enters the sixth (gate). It emerges and sets through the sixth gate for thirty-one[c] days because of its sign. 14/ During that day the daytime grows longer than the night, with the daytime being double the night. The daytime is twelve parts, while the night grows shorter and is six parts. 15/ The sun rises so that the daytime becomes shorter and the night longer; the sun returns to the east and enters the sixth gate. It rises from it and sets for thirty days. 16/ When the thirty days are completed, daytime decreases one part exactly; the daytime is eleven parts and the night seven. 17/ The sun emerges from the west from that sixth gate, goes to the east, and rises in the fifth gate for thirty mornings. It again sets in the west, in the fifth western gate. 18/ On that day the daytime is two parts fewer, with the daytime being ten parts and the night eight parts. 19/ The sun emerges from that fifth gate and sets through the fifth gate in the west; it rises through the fourth gate because of its

----

a Lit. *from.*

b Lit. *double, doubling; twofold.* The reference is to two of the eighteen units in a day, that is, one-ninth.

c Several mss lack the number *one,* thus reading *thirty.*

sign[a]—in the fourth gate in the east[b]—thirty-one mornings and sets in the west. 20/ On that day the daytime is equal to the night; it is the same: the night is nine parts and the daytime nine parts as well. 21/ The sun emerges from that gate and sets in the west; it returns to the east and emerges through the third gate for thirty mornings and sets in the west through the third gate. 22/ On that day the night is longer than the daytime; night becomes longer than night, day becomes shorter than day for thirty days. The night is ten parts exactly and the daytime eight parts. 23/ The sun emerges from that third gate and sets through the third gate in the west; it returns to the east and emerges through the second gate in the east for thirty mornings; in the same way it sets through the second gate on the west side of the sky. 24/ On that day the night is eleven parts and the daytime seven parts. 25/ The sun emerges on that day from that second gate and sets in the west through the second gate. It returns to the east in the first gate for thirty-one mornings[c] and sets through the first gate in the west.[d] 26/ On that day the night is longer and is double the daytime; the night is twelve parts exactly and the daytime six parts. 27/ The sun has completed the chief points of its (route). It again goes about on those chief points of its (route) and enters each gate[e] for thirty mornings, and it sets in the west opposite it. 28/ On that day[f] the night decreases in length by a ninth part, that is, one part and is a night of eleven parts and a daytime of seven parts. 29/ The sun returned and entered[g] the second gate on the east. It returns upon those chief points

---

a Some mss read a plural form.

b *In the fourth gate in the east*: some mss omit these words.

c A few mss add *because of its sign*.

d Some mss lack *in the west* (some place these words before *through the first gate*); others add *of the sky*.

e Variants include *that gate; all its gates*.

f Some mss read *night*.

g *Returned and entered*: the mss read perfect tense forms of the verbs, though imperfect tense forms are the norm elsewhere in this solar table.

of its (route); for thirty days it rises and sets. 30/ On that day the night decreases in length (relative to the daytime), with the night being ten parts and the daytime eight parts. 31/ On that day the sun emerges from that[a] gate and sets in the west; it returns to the east and rises through the third gate for thirty-one mornings and sets on the west side of the sky. 32/ On that day the night decreases and is nine parts, with a daytime of nine parts. Daytime is equal to the night, and the year is exactly 364 days. 33/ The length of the daytime and the night and the shortness of the daytime and the night vary during the course of the sun. 34/ For this reason its course grows longer day by day and night by night it grows shorter.

35   This is the law and course of the sun: its return when it returns sixty times and emerges. It is the great luminary which is called the sun forever. 36/ This one that emerges is the great luminary, and it is named after its appearance as the Lord commanded. 37/ In this way it emerges and so it enters; it neither decreases nor rests but runs day and night.[b] Its light is seven times brighter than that of the moon, but the size of the two is equal.

The Law of the Phases of the Moon (Chapter 73)

73:1   After this law I saw a second law for the smaller luminary whose name is the moon. 2/ Its roundness is like the roundness of the sky,[c] and the wind blows its chariot on which it rides, with light being given to it in measure. 3/ Each month its emergence and setting change, and its days are like the days of the sun. When its light is evenly distributed (over its surface), it is one-seventh the light of the sun. 4/ In this way it rises with its beginning toward the east; it emerges on the thirtieth day, and on that day it is visible. It becomes for you

_____

a Some mss add *second.*

b Some mss add *in a chariot.*

c Some mss read *sun.*

the beginning of the month on the thirtieth day with the sun in the gate where the sun emerges. 5[a] / Its half is distant one-seventh part (from the sun?), and all its disc is empty, with no light except its seventh part, one-fourteenth part of its light. 6/ During the day it takes on a seventh part of half its light (i.e., one-fourteenth) and its illuminated section is a

---

a 73:5-8 offer a text with many difficulties, a fact reflected in the numerous variants in the mss. The writer appears to be describing the illuminated portions of the moon's surface (that is, the half of the moon facing the earth) on the first two days of a lunar month. As the Aramaic copies show, he was severely abbreviating a lengthier table which supplied such information for a much longer time, possibly even an entire year. He was also working with two fractions: the moon's light, when full, is 1/7 that of the sun; and the half of the lunar surface facing the earth is segmented into fourteenths. An additional 1/14 is illuminated each day during its waxing and darkened during its waning. The table is more fully expressed in the Aramaic copies. Part of the Aramaic text which may correspond to this section of the Ethiopic version is given here.

4Q209 Fragment 7 ii

2 [it remains during this day four and one-half sevenths; then it sets and enters and is covered the rest] of this day

3 [two and one-half] sevenths. *blank* [During the twenty-fourth night] in it it is covered four and one-half sevenths and there is subtracted from its light

4 [four and one-half sevenths. T]hen it goes out and shines during the rest of this night two and one-half sevenths. It remains

5 [during] this [d]ay five sevenths. Then it sets and enters and is covered the rest of this day two sevenths. *blank*

6 During the twenty-fifth night in it it is covered five sevenths and there is subtracted from its light five sevenths.

7 Then it goes out and shines during the rest of this night two sevenths and remains during this day five and one-half sevenths.

8 Then it sets [and] enters the second gate and is covered the rest of this day one and one-half sevenths. *blank*

9 During the twenty-sixth night in it it is covered five and one-half sevenths, and there is subtracted from its light five and one-half sevenths.

10 Then it emerges from the second gate and shines during the rest of this night one and one-half sevenths, and it remains during this day

11 six sevenths. Then it sets and enters and is covered the rest of this day one seventh. *blank* During the [twen]ty-seventh night

12 in it it is covered six sevenths, and there is subtracted from its [li]ght [six] sev[enths. Then it emerges and shines]

13 [the res]t of this night one seventh, and it remains during this day [six and one-half sevenths. Then it sets and enters]

half seventh part.[a] 7/ It sets with the sun, and when the sun rises it rises with it and receives a half part of light. During that night, at the beginning of its day, at the beginning of the moon's day, the moon sets with the sun and is dark that night six[b] seventh parts and a half. 8/ It rises during that day (with) a seventh part exactly. It emerges and recedes from the rising of the sun and is bright in the rest of its day six seventh parts.

Another Law of the Moon (Chapter 74)

74:1[c]   Another course and[d] law I saw for it; by that law it carries out its monthly course. 2/ All this Uriel the holy angel who is the leader of them all[e] showed me. Their positions I wrote down as he showed me and I wrote down their months as they were and the appearance of their light until fifteen days were completed. 3/ In one-seventh parts it completes[f] all its light in the east and in the west. 4/ In certain months it changes (the places of) its settings, and in certain months it goes its own way. 5/ During two months it sets with the sun in those two middle gates—in the third and in the fourth gate. 6/ It emerges for seven days, goes around, and returns again to the gate from which the sun emerges; it completes all its light, recedes from the sun, and enters for eight days into the sixth gate from which the sun emerges. 7/ When the sun emerges from the fourth gate, (the moon) emerges for seven days

---

a Half seventh part: one would expect such a statement, but the mss read a variety of other numerical expressions.

b Some mss read *seven.*

c 4Q209 Frg. 25 may correspond with 74:1-2 (or 78:9?):

1 [   ] the years [
2 [   ] *blank* [
3 [   ] another [cal]culation I was shown for it that it went [
4 [   ] . [   ] months [

d Many mss lack *and.*

e Many mss add *and their positions.*

f Some mss add *all its darkness and in one-seventh parts completes.*

until it emerges from the fifth; it again returns in seven days into the fourth gate and completes all its light. It recedes and enters into the first gate for eight days. 8/ It again returns in seven days into the fourth gate from which the sun emerges. 9/ In this way I saw their positions, as the moon rises and the sun sets during those days.

10   When five years are added up, the total comes to thirty (extra) days for the sun. All the days that result for one of those five years, when complete, are 364 days. 11/ The extra amount for the sun and stars comes to six days; for five years six (extra) days come to thirty days, and the moon is thirty days less than the sun and the stars, 12/ and they bring about the year precisely, all according to their eternal positions. They come neither early nor late by one day by which they would change the year: each is exactly 364 days. 13/ In three years there are 1,092 days; in five years there are 1,820 days, with the result that in eight years there are 2,912. 14/ For the moon alone, the days in three years come to 1,062; in five years it is fifty days fewer.[a] 15/ In five years there are 1,770 days with the result that in eight years the moon has 2,832 days. 16/ For in eight years eighty days are lacking; all the days that it lacks after eight years are eighty days. 17/ Then the year is correctly completed in accord with their eternal positions and the positions of the sun; they rise from the gate from which it rises and sets for 30 days.

The Leaders and the Seasons (75:1-3)

75:1   The leaders of the heads of the thousands who are over all the creation and over all the stars (have to do) with those four (days) that are added; they are not separated from their position[b] according to the calculation of the year, and they serve

---

a Many mss add words that may mean: *after/at the end of the number 62 in the text one makes an addition and it becomes.*

b Some mss read *its/their work.*

on the four days that are not reckoned in the calculation of the year. 2/ People err regarding them because those lights truly serve (in) the position of the world: one in the first gate, one in the third heavenly gate, one in the fourth gate, and one in the sixth gate, and the accuracy of the world is completed[a] in the 364 positions of the world. 3/ For Uriel the angel whom the Lord of eternal glory set[b] over all the heavenly luminaries, in the sky and in the world, showed me the sign, the seasons, the year and the days so that they may rule the firmament, appear above the earth, and be leaders of days and nights—the sun, the moon, the stars, and all the serving entities that go around in all the heavenly chariots.

Twelve Gates, Windows, and Chariots (75:4-9)

4   In the same way Uriel showed me twelve gates open in the disc of the sun's chariot in the sky from which the rays of the sun come out and from which its heat comes out upon the earth when they are opened at the times stipulated for them. 5/[c] 6/ The same is the case when the twelve gates are opened[d] in the sky on the boundaries of the earth, from which the sun, the moon, the stars, and all the works of the sky emerge, on the east and on the west. 7/ There are many windows opened on the left and right. Each window at its time emits heat like those gates from which the stars emerge as he ordered them and in which they set according to their number. 8/ I saw chariots in the sky traveling in the world above[e] those gates in which the stars that do not set revolve. 9/ One is larger than all of them and it is the one that encircles the whole world.

---

a Some mss read *it will complete.*

b Some mss add *forever.*

c The entire v. 5 appears to be the result of textual errors and for this reason has been omitted from the translation.

d Some mss omit *when . . . are opened* and read *I saw.*

e Some mss add *and below.*

The Twelve Winds and Their Gates (Chapter 76)

76:1   At the boundaries of the earth I saw twelve gates open for all
        the winds, from which the winds emerge and blow on the
        earth. 2/ Three of them are open in front of the sky, three on
        the west, three on the right of the sky, and three on the left.
        3ᵃ/ The first three are toward the east, three toward the north;
        the three after theseᵇ on the left are toward the south and three
        on the west. 4/ Through four of them emerge winds of bless-
        ing and peace, but, from those (other) eight, winds of pun-
        ishment emerge; when they are sent they bring devastation to
        the entire earth and the water on it, all that live on it, and all
        that are in the water and on the land. 5/ The first wind, whose
        name is "eastern," emerges from those gates through the first
        gate which is on the east and inclines toward the south; from
        it there emerge devastation, drought, heat, and destruction.
        6/ Through the second gate, the middle one, there emerge in
        a direct wayᶜ rain, fruitfulness, prosperity, and dew; through
        the third gate which is to the north emerge cold and drought.
        7/ Following these the winds toward the south emerge
        through three gates. First, through the first gate that inclines
        toward the east a hot wind emerges. 8/ Through the middle

---

    a For 76:3-10, 13 (?)-14 two Aram copies preserve a number of words and phrases.
For 76:3-10 4Q210 frg. 1 ii 1-10 offers the following:

1   and three after them on the left. *blank* [
2   and for the healing of the earth and for revivifying it. *blank* And [
3   and the waters and everything in them which grow and sprout and creep [
4   through the first gate there emerges an east wind which is in [the east
5   through the second gate there emerges an eas[tern] east wind [
6   a northeastern [wind] which is close to the nor[th] wind [
7   there emerges at first through the first gate [
8   which they call South; dew [
9   [and] after it the n[orth] wind emerges [
10   [destr]uction. *blank* [

    b Some mss read *opposite these.*

    c Some mss add *and there emerge,* but the extra words do not fit the pattern in this
section. Cf. 76:11.

gate next to it there emerge a fragrant aroma, dew, rain, prosperity, and life. 9/ Through the third gate that is toward the west there emerge dew, rain, locusts, and destruction. 10/ Following these the winds that are toward the north, whose name is "sea," and which emerge from[a] the seventh gate that is toward the southeast—there emerge from it dew, rain, locust, destruction. 11/ From the middle gate in a direct way there emerge life, rain, dew; through the third gate that is toward the west, inclining to the north, there emerge mist, hail, snow, rain, dew, and locust. 12/ Following these (there are) four winds[b] which are toward the west: (as for) the first gate toward the north, from it emerge dew,[c] hail, cold, snow, frost. 13[d]/ From the middle gate there emerge dew, rain, prosperity, and blessing. From the last gate that is toward the south emerge drought, destruction, burning, and devastation. 14/ The twelve gates of the four quarters[e] of the sky are completed. All their laws and all their punishment and their prosperity—I have shown to you everything, my son Methuselah.

---

a Many mss add *three*.

b The number appears wrong, though it is attested in all the Eth mss. Three winds are enumerated for each quarter, not four.

c Some mss add *and rain*.

d Two Aram copies, 4Q209 frg. 23 1-2 and 4Q210 1 ii 14, include some words from 76:13-14. Combining the two copies, one can read:

76:13] and devastation. 76:14 The twelve gates of the four quarters of the sky are completed. Their prosperity and their interpretation I have [shown …

e The Eth mss read *gates*, but Aram has *quarters*.

The Four Quarters of the Earth,
Its Seven Mountains and Seven Rivers (Chapter 77)

77:1[a]   The first quarter is called "eastern" because it is the first; and
the second is called "south" because there the Most High
will descend and especially there the one who is blessed forever will descend. 2/ The name of the quarter on the west
is "diminished" because there all the heavenly luminaries
diminish and go down. 3/ The fourth quarter whose name
is "north" is divided into three parts. One of them is the
place where people live; the second is for the seas, the deeps,
forests, rivers, darkness, and mist; and the other[b] part is for
the garden of righteousness. 4/ I saw seven lofty mountains
which are higher than all the mountains on the earth; from
them snow emerges, and days, seasons, and years pass by.[c]
5/ I saw seven[d] rivers on the earth, larger than all the rivers. One of them comes from the west (and) pours its water
into the great sea. 6/ Two of them come from the north to
the sea and pour their water into the Erythrean Sea on the
east. 7/ The remaining four emerge on the northern side
toward their sea, <two>[e] into the Erythrean Sea and two[f]

---

a 4Q209 23 3-10 and 4Q210 1 ii [14]-20 preserve parts of 77:1-4. The combined
text reads:

77:1 [The east is called "east" because it is] the first. The south is called "south"
because there the Great One lives and in (?) [ ] forever. *blank* 77:2 The great quarter (is
called) the western quarter because there [ ] the heavenly [st]ars [come], and hundreds/
vessels set and hundreds/ vessels enter, and all of them are stars. For this reason it is
called "the west." 77:3 [The north (is called) "north"] because in it all the entities that
set hide, gather, and go around; they go to the east side of the sky ["ea]st" because from
there the vessels of the sky rise; and also "orient" because from there/ hundreds rise
[ ] the earth. One of them serves as a place where people live, and one of them [ ] for
deserts. And for [the gard]en of righteousness. *bla[nk* 77:4 I saw sev]en mo[untains
higher than a]ll mo[untains on the ea]r[th, and] snow [ca]me down on them [

b Many mss read *third*.

c Some mss add *and go*.

d Some mss omit *seven*.

e The sense requires this addition, though no ms reads this word.

f A couple of mss read *four*.

into the great sea where they empty themselves, but some say into the wilderness. 8/ I saw seven large islands in the sea and on the land—five on the land and two in the Erythrean Sea.[a]

The Sun and the Moon and the Waxing and Waning of the Moon (Chapter 78)

78:1   The names of the sun are as follows: the first Aryares and the second Tomas. 2/ The moon has four names: its first name is Asanya, the second Abla, the third Banase, and the fourth Era. 3/ These are the two great luminaries. Their roundness is like the roundness of the sky, and the size[b] of the two of them is the same. 4/ In the disc of the sun there are seven parts of light added to it beyond what the moon has; a specific amount is placed (in the moon) until the seventh part of the sun passes over. 5/ They set and enter the gates of the west and go around the north and emerge through the gates of the east on the firmament.

6[c]/   When the moon rises, it is visible in the sky (with) one-half of a seventh part of all its light; on the fourteenth it completes its light. 7/ Fifteen parts of light are placed in it until its light is completed in fifteen (days) for the sign of the year. It is in fifteen parts, while the moon grows by (units of) one-half

---

a Some mss have *great sea* and some show variations in the numbers.

b Some mss add *of their roundness is like the roundness of the sky.*

c 4Q210 1 iii 3-8 corresponds with 78:6-8 and reads as follows:

3 [shi]ned in the sky to appe[ar

4 [and are com]plete each and every day until the fourteenth day and are com[plete]

5 [   ] fifteen and all its light is complete in it

6 [   ] and it leads the moons by halves of sevenths *blank* [

7 [   ] and in the second day one of thir[teen

8 [   ] one of ele[ven

of a seventh part. 8/ When it is waning, on the first day it decreases to fourteen parts of its light, and on the next day it decreases to thirteen parts of light. On the third it decreases to twelve, on the fourth to eleven parts, on the fifth it decreases to ten parts, on the sixth it decreases to nine parts, on the seventh it decreases to eight parts, on the eighth it decreases to seven, on the ninth it decreases to six, on the tenth it decreases to five, on the eleventh it decreases to four, on the twelfth it decreases to three, on the thirteenth it decreases to two[a], on the fourteenth it decreases to one-half of a seventh part of all its light, and on the fifteenth day the entire remainder is exhausted. 9/ During certain months the moon has 29 days and sometimes 28.

10/   Uriel showed me another law: (regarding) when the light is placed in the moon and from where it is placed (in the moon) from the sun.[b] 11/ The entire time the moon progresses it adds its light when facing the sun until in fourteen days its light is complete.[c] When it is all aflame its light is complete in the sky. 12/ On the first day it is called the new moon because on that day the light rises on it. 13/ It is complete precisely on the day the sun sets in the west and it rises from the east during the night and the moon shines during the entire night, until the sun rises opposite it and the moon is seen[d] opposite the sun. 14/ From the place where the light comes to the moon, from there again it decreases until all the light is exhausted. A lunar day passes and its disc remains empty without light. 15/ It fashions three months of thirty days in its times; when it effects its decrease it fashions three months of twenty-nine days each, during which it brings about its decrease in the first time (period) and in the first gate, in 177 days. 16/ When it goes out it appears for three months, each with thirty days, and three months it appears, each with twenty-nine days. 17[e]/ At night it appears every twenty (days) like a man, and at

---

a Some mss read *one-half.*

b Some mss read *from the east.*

c Some mss add *in the sky.*

d Some mss read *is equal.*

e 4Q209 Frg. 26 corresponds with material in 79:3-5; 78:17—79:2 and reads this way:

daytime like the sky because there is nothing else in it except its light.

A Summary (Chapter 79)

79:1   Now my son[a] I have shown you everything, and the law of all the stars of the sky is completed. 2/ He showed me all their law for each day, each time in a[b] jurisdiction, every year, its emergence, the command, every month, and every week; 3/ the decrement of the moon which is accomplished in the sixth gate because in this sixth gate its light is completed and from it comes the beginning of the decrement 4/ which is accomplished in the first gate at its time until 177 days are completed, by the law of the week twenty-five (weeks) and two days. 5/ It[c] falls behind the sun and in relation to the law of the stars five days exactly in one period and when this place which you see is completed. 6/ This is the appearance and the likeness of each luminary that Uriel, the great angel who is their leader, showed me.

Uriel's Summary and Prediction of Human Sin and Its Consequences (Chapter 80)

80:1   At that time Uriel the angel[d] responded to me: "I have now shown you everything, Enoch, and I have revealed every-

---

1 [   ] ... [

2 [   ] through the sixth gate . . [

3 [25 weeks and] two [d]ays. There was a lack in relation to the sun [

4 [   ] . . . in it like the image of a mirror when (one) has shin[ed] its light on it [

5 [in the night for] part (of the time); this appearance resembles the likeness of a man, and during the day for [part...]

6 its [light] alone. Now I am telling you, my son. *blank* [

7 [   ] a calculation. He showed m[e

   a Some mss add *Methuselah*.

   b Some mss read (*and*) *in every*.

   c Some mss read *And how*.

   d Some mss omit *the angel*.

thing to you so that you may see this sun and this moon and those who lead the stars of the sky and all those who turn them—their work, their times, and their emergences.

2 In the days of the sinners the rainy seasons will grow shorter,
      their seed will become late on their land and in their fields.
   Everything on the earth will change
      and will not appear at their times,
   the rain will be withheld,
      and the sky will stand still.[a]

3 At those times the fruit of the earth will be late and will not
         grow at its normal time,
      and the fruit of the trees will be withheld at its (normal)
         time.

4 The moon will change its order[b]
      and will not appear at its (normal) time.

5 At that time it will appear in the sky[c]
      and will arrive at . . .[d] at the edge of the great chariot in
         the west
      and will shine very much more (brightly) than its normal
         light.

6 Many heads of the stars will stray from the command[e]
      and will change their ways and actions
      and will not appear at the times prescribed for them.

7 The entire law of the stars will be closed to the sinners,
      and the thoughts of those on the earth will err regarding
         them.
   They will turn back from all their ways,
      will err, and will take them to be gods.

8 Evil will multiply against them
      and punishment will come upon them to destroy all."

---

a Some mss read a causative form of the verb.
b Or *law.*
c Some mss read *the sky will appear.*
d The mss read *famine/ drought* here, but the word is curious in the context.
e Some mss read *stars of the command.*

Enoch Views the Heavenly Tablets and Returns to Earth (Chapter 81)

81:1   He said to me: "Enoch, look at these[a] heavenly tablets, read what is written on them, and understand each and every item." 2/ I looked at everything on the heavenly tablets, read everything that was written, and understood everything. I read the book, all[b] the actions of people and of all humans who will be on the earth for the generations of the world. 3/ From that time forward I blessed the great[c] Lord, the king of glory forever, as he had made every work of the world. I praised the Lord because of his patience; I blessed (him) on account of humanity.[d] 4/ Afterwards[e] I said: "Blessed is the one who dies righteous and good; regarding him no book of wickedness has been written and no day of judgment[f] will be found."[g] 5/ Those seven[h] holy ones brought me and set me on the earth in front of the gate to my house. They said to me: "Tell everything to your son Methuselah and show all your children that no human is righteous before the Lord, for he created them. 6/ We will leave you with your son[i] for one year until (you receive) another order,[j] to teach your children and write for them, and you will testify to all your children; in the second year they will take you from them. 7/ May your heart be strong because the good will inform the good of righteousness, the righteous will rejoice with the righteous, and they will greet each other. 8/ But the sinner

----

a Some mss add *books of the.*

b Some mss read *the book and everything written in it, all.*

c Some mss lack *great.*

d Some mss read (literally) *the children of (all) the world* or *all the generations of the world.*

e Some mss read *At the time.*

f Some mss read *on the day of judgment*; others read *error against him.*

g Some mss read *has been found.*

h Some mss read *three.*

i Some mss read *sons/ children.*

j One ms reads *you again comfort him.* For an alternative translation, see Knibb, *Enoch* 2, 187.

will die with the sinner and the apostate will drown with the apostate. 9/ Those who do what is right will die because of the actions of people and will be gathered up because of the deeds of the wicked." 10/ At that time they finished speaking with me and I went to my people blessing the Lord of the world.[a]

Enoch's Instruction to Methuselah (82:1-3)

82:1   Now my son Methuselah, I am telling you all these things and am writing (them) down.[b] I have revealed all of them to you and have given you the books about all these things. My son,[c] keep the book written by[d] your father so that you may give (it) to the generations[e] of the world. 2/ Wisdom I have given to you and to your children[f] and to those who will be your children so that they may give this wisdom which is beyond their thought to their children for the generations. 3/ Those who understand will not sleep and will listen with their ear to learn this wisdom. It will be more pleasing to them than fine food to those who eat.

Right and Wrong Calendrical Practice
An Assertion of the Truth of Enoch's Account (82:4-8)

4   Blessed are all the righteous, all the blessed[g] who will walk in the way of righteousness and have no sin like the sinners in numbering all the days the sun travels in the sky through the gates, entering and emerging for thirty days with the heads of thousands of the order of the stars, with the four addi-

---

a Some mss read *of the ages.*
b Some mss add *for you.*
c Some mss add *Methuselah.*
d Lit. *from the hand of.*
e Some mss read *the children.*
f A few mss read *your son.*
g Some mss omit all or part of *all the blessed.*

tional ones that divide[a] between the four parts of the year that lead them and enter with the four days. 5/ People err regarding them and do not calculate them in the numbering of the entire year because they err regarding them and people do not understand them precisely. 6/ For they belong in the reckoning of the year and are indeed recorded forever: one in the first gate, one in the third, one in the fourth, and one in the sixth. Thus a year of 364 days is completed.[b] 7/ The account about it is true and its calculation is precisely recorded because the luminaries and the months, the festivals, the years, and the days he showed me, and Uriel, to whom the Lord of the entire creation gave orders for me regarding the host of heaven, breathed on me. 8/ He has power in heaven over night and day to make light appear over humanity: the sun, the moon, the stars, and all the heavenly powers which revolve in their circuits.

The Law of the Stars, Their Leaders, and the Four Seasons (82:9-20)

9[c]   This is the law of the stars which set in their places, at their times, at their set times, and in their months. 10/ These are the names of those who lead them, who keep watch so they enter at their times, who lead them in their places,[d] in their orders, in their times, in their months, in their jurisdictions, and in their positions. 11/ Their four leaders who divide the

---

a Some mss read *are divided.*

b Some mss read *a year is completed in 364 days.*

c 4Q209 Frg. 28 corresponds with 82:9-13 and reads this way:

1 [for] their festivals, for their months for their signs. And [
2 [and according to] their [r]ule for all their stations. Fo[ur
3 [   ] heads o[f] [
4 [div]iding among d[ays
5 [th]ese are the names of [

d Some mss lack *who lead them in their places.*

four parts of the year enter first, and after them (come) the
twelve leaders of the orders who divide the months, and[a]
the 360 heads of thousands who separate the days, and the
four additional ones with them are the leaders who separate
the four parts of the years.[b] 12/ (As for) these heads of thousands between leader and leader,[c] one is added behind the
position and their leaders make a division. 13/ These are the
names of the leaders who separate the four fixed parts of the
year: Milkiel, Helememelek, Mele'eyel, and Narel. 14/ The
names of those whom they lead (are): Adnare'el, Iyasusael,
and Elome'el; these three follow the leaders of the orders,
and one follows the three leaders of the orders who follow
those leaders of the positions who separate the four parts of
the year. 15/ At the beginning of the year[d] Melkeyal rises first
and rules—the one called the southern[e] sun; all the days that
fall within the period that he rules are 91 days. 16/ These
are the signs of the days that are to be seen on the earth
during the days of his rule: sweat, heat, and care;[f] all the
trees bear fruit and leaves come out on all the trees; (there
is) a harvest of wheat, roses, and all the flowers that bloom
in the field; but the winter trees are dried up. 17/ These are
the names of the leaders who are beneath them: Berka'el,
Zelebesel, and another head of a thousand who is added has
the name Hiluyasef. His days of rule are completed. 18/ A
second leader after him[g] is Helememelek who is named the
bright sun; all the days of his light are 91 days. 19/ These
are the signs of the days[h] on the earth: heat, drought, trees
bearing their fruit ripe and yielding all their fruit ripe and
ready;[i] the sheep mate and become pregnant; people gather

---

a Some mss add *and the year(s) into 364 days with.*

b Some mss read *its four parts.*

c Some mss read *leader and the one led.*

d Some mss omit *of the year.*

e A transliteration of the word *southern* (*taymani*) is used.

f One ms reads *calm.*

g Some mss read *them.*

h Some mss read *the days of* (*his*) *sign.*

i Some mss read (*and*) *it is dry.*

all the fruit of the earth and everything in the fields and the winepress—it happens during the days of his rule. 20/ These are the names, the orders, and the leaders[a] of those heads of thousands: Gida'iyal, Ke'el, and He'el;[b] the name of one who is added to them as a head of thousands[c] is Asfa'el, and the days of his rule are completed.[d]

---

a Some mss add *who are under them.*

b Some mss omit *He'el.*

c Some mss add *his name.*

d Although the section beginning at 82:15 should contain descriptions of each of the four parts of the year—one for each of the four leaders mentioned in 82:13—the text includes only the first two and then abruptly breaks off. It is possible that 4Q211 Frg. 1 i-iii preserves part of the lost ending of the book. This is the text as it has survived:

i
1 [   ] ....
2 [dew] and rain they make fall [o]n the earth and seed
3 [   ] plants of the earth and trees and it emerges and enters
4 [   ] . and it becomes winter, and the leaves of all the trees
5 [four]teen trees for which it is not fitting
6 [   ] ... remain
ii
1 [   ]
2 this from its measure [   ]
3 tenth of on[e-]ninth [   ]
4 one-ninth and sta[rs] went out (?) through [the] fir[st   ] of the sky; [then] they
     went out
5 on the first day [one-] tenth [by] one-[six]th and the second (day) one of fifteen
6 by on[e-] sixth [and] the third day on[e o]f thirty by one-sixth   *blank*
7 [   ]
iii
1 [   ]
2 [   ]
3 [   ]
4 on [the fif]te[enth day] . [   ] in its sign (?) in [the] da[y]
5 but [in] this night [a th]ird of a ninth and fiv[e   ]
6 and ten of a ninth   *blank*   [   ]
7 [   ]

Enoch's Dream Visions

(Chapters 83–90)

Enoch's First Dream Vision:
The Flood (Chapters 83–84)

83:1   And now, my son Methuselah, I will show you all the visions
      that I saw;
        before you I will recount (them).

2   Two visions I saw before I took a wife,
      and the one was unlike the other.
    The first (was) when I was learning to write,
      and the second, before I took your mother (as my wife).
    I saw a terrible vision,
      and concerning it I made supplication to the Lord.

3   I was lying down in the house of Mahalalel, my grandfather,
      (when) I saw in a vision.
    Heaven was thrown down and taken away,
      and it fell down upon the earth.

4   And when it fell upon the earth,
      I saw how the earth was swallowed up in the great abyss.
    Mountains were suspended upon mountains,
      and hills sank down upon hills;
    Tall trees were cut from their roots,
      and were thrown away and sank into the abyss.

5   And then speech fell into my mouth, and I lifted up (my
      voice) to cry out and said,
    "The earth has been destroyed."

6   And Mahalalel my grandfather aroused me, since I was lying
      near him, and said to me,

"Why do you cry out so, my son,
  and why do you lament so?"

7 And I recounted to him the whole vision that I had seen, and
      he said to me,
  "A terrible thing you have seen, my son,
    and mighty is the vision of your dream (in) the secrets of
      all the sin of the earth.
  It must sink into the abyss,
    and it will be utterly destroyed.

8 And now, my son, arise and make supplication to the Lord of
      glory, since you are faithful,
  that a remnant may remain upon the earth,
    and that he may not obliterate the whole earth.

9 My son, from heaven all this will take place on the earth,
    and on the earth there will be great destruction."

10 Then I arose and prayed and made supplication and request,
    and my prayer I wrote down for the generations of eter-
      nity,
    and everything I shall show you, my son Methuselah.

11 And when I went out below,
    and saw the heaven and the sun rising in the east,
    and the moon setting in the west and a few stars,
    and all the earth and everything as he <made>[a] it from the
      beginning,
  Then I blessed the Lord of judgment, and to him I ascribed
      majesty,
    for he made the sun go forth from the windows of the
      east,
    so that it ascended and rose on the face of the heaven,
    and he made it rise, and it traverses the path that it was
      shown.

---

a Eth *knew*, evidently corrupt. See Charles, *Eth. Enoch*, 161, n. 12.

84:1   And I lifted up my hands in righteousness and blessed the
               Great Holy One,
           and I spoke with the breath of my mouth and with a
               tongue of flesh,**ᵃ**
           which God has made for the sons of the flesh of man, that
               they might speak with it.
           {And he has given them breath and tongue and mouth
               that they might speak with it.}**ᵇ**
2   "Blessed are you, O Lord, King,
           great and mighty in your majesty,
           Lord of all the creation of the heaven,
           King of kings and God of all eternity.
        Your power and your reign and your majesty abide forever
               and forever and ever,
           and to all generations, your dominion.
        All the heavens are your throne forever,
           and all the earth is your footstool forever and forever and
               ever.
3   For you have made and you rule all things,
           and nothing is too difficult for you;
        Wisdom does not escape you,
           <and it does not turn away from your throne,>**ᶜ** nor from
               your presence.
        You know and see and hear all things,
           and there is nothing that is hidden from you.**ᵈ**
4   And now the angels of your heavens are doing wrong,
           and upon human flesh is your wrath until the great day of
               judgment.
5   And now, O God and Lord and great King,

---

a I.e, a human tongue. *flesh* retained here to indicate parallels in vv 1c, 4b, 6a.
b Line appears to be a doublet of the previous one.
c For the emendation and the textual problems behind it, see *1 Enoch 1*, 346.
d All Eth mss add *for you see all things*, almost certainly a doublet of previous line.

I make supplication and request that you fulfill my prayer,
    to leave me a remnant on the earth,
    and not obliterate all human flesh,
    and devastate the earth,
    that there be eternal destruction.

6   And now, my Lord, remove from the earth the flesh that has
        aroused your wrath,
    but the righteous and true flesh raise up as a seed-bearing
        plant forever.
And hide not your face from the prayer of your servant, O
    Lord."

Enoch's Second Dream Vision: The History of Humanity (Chapters 85–90)

Introduction to the Vision

85:1   After this I saw a second dream, and I will show all of it to
        you, my son.

2   And Enoch lifted up (his voice) and said to his son Methu-
        selah, "To you I speak, my son. Hear my words, and
        incline your ear to the dream vision of your father.

From Adam to the Fall of Jerusalem

Adam and Eve and Their Children

3   Before I took your mother Edna (as my wife), I saw in a vision
        on my bed, and look, a bull came forth from the earth, and
        that bull was white. And after it a young heifer came forth.
        And with her two bull calves came forth; one of them was
        black, and one was red. 4/ And that black calf struck the red
        one and †pursued it over the earth.†[a] And from then on I

---

a The order *struck* and *pursued* is odd. Perhaps the verbs should be reversed, or the
second verb should be passive: Cain is pursued. See *1 Enoch 1*, 371.

could not see that red calf. 5/ But that black calf grew up, and a young heifer came to it. And I saw that many cattle came forth from it, that were like it and were following after it. 6/ And that female calf, that first one, went forth from the presence of that first bull; she searched for that red calf, but did not find it, and she lamented bitterly over it and searched for it. 7/ And I looked until that first bull came to her and quieted her, and from that time on she did not cry out. 8/ After this she bore another white bull, and after it she bore many black bulls and cows.

9   And I saw in my sleep that white bull, that it grew likewise and became a large white bull, and from it came forth many white cattle, and they were like it. 10/ And they began to bear many white cattle, which were like them, and each one followed the other.

*The Fall of the Watchers and
the Violence of the Giants*

86:1   And again I saw with my eyes as I was sleeping. I saw the heaven above, and look, a star fell from heaven, and it arose and was eating and pasturing among those cattle.[a] 2/ Then I saw those large and black cattle, and look, all of them exchanged their pens and their pastures and their calves, and they began to moan,[b] one after the other.

3   And again I saw in the vision, and I looked to heaven, and look, I saw many stars descend and cast themselves down from heaven to that first star. And in the midst of those calves they became bulls, and they were pasturing with them in their midst.[c] 4/ I looked at them and I saw and look, all of them let out their organs like horses, and they began to mount the cows of the bulls, and they all conceived and bore elephants and camels and asses. 5/ And all

---

a Fragmentary Aram *among them* indicates a somewhat different wording.
b This verb attested in only one Eth ms, but see *1 Enoch 1*, 367.
c Precise translation of this verse uncertain. See *1 Enoch 1*, 367.

the bulls feared them and were terrified before them, and they began to bite with their teeth and devour and gore with their horns. 6/ And they began to devour those bulls, and look, all the sons of the earth began to tremble and quake before them, and to flee.

Divine Judgment

87:1   And again I saw them, and they began to gore one another and devour one another, and the earth began to cry out. 2/ And I lifted my eyes again to heaven, and I saw in the vision, and look, there came forth from heaven (beings) with the appearance of white men; four came forth from that place and three with them. 3/ And those three who came after took hold of me by my hand and raised me from the generations of the earth, and lifted me onto a high place, and they showed me a tower high above the earth, and all the hills were smaller. 4/ And they said to me, 'Stay here until you see all that happens to those elephants and camels and asses and to the stars and to the cattle and all of them.'

88:1   And I saw one of those four who had come before; he seized that first star that had fallen from heaven, and he bound it by its hands and feet and threw it into an abyss, and that abyss was narrow and deep and desolate and dark.ᵃ 2/ And one of these drew a sword and gave it to those elephants and camels and asses. And they began to strike one another, and the whole earth quaked because of them. 3/ And as I looked in the vision, look, one of those four who had come forth hurled stones from heaven and gathered and took all the great stars, whose organs were like the organs of horses, and bound all of them by their hands and their feet, and threw them into an abyss of the earth.

---

a Eth *darkness*, perhaps an Aram adjective has been corrupted to a noun.

Noah and the Flood

89:1   And one of those four went to <one of the white bulls>[a] and
         taught it a mystery—trembling as it was.[b] It was born a bull
         but became a man. And he built himself a vessel[c] and dwelt
         in it, and three bulls dwelt with him on that vessel, and the
         vessel was covered and roofed over them.[d] 2/ And again I
         lifted my eyes toward heaven, and I saw a high roof and
         seven sluices on it, and those sluices were pouring out much
         water into an enclosure. 3/ And I looked again and look,
         fissures opened up in the floor in that large enclosure, and
         that water began to bubble up and rise above the floor, and I
         was looking at that enclosure until all the floor was covered
         with water. 4/ And water and darkness and mist increased
         on it, and I kept seeing the height of that water, and that
         water had risen above that enclosure and was overflowing
         that enclosure and stood on the earth. 5/ And all the cattle
         of that enclosure were gathered together until I saw them
         sinking and being engulfed and perishing in that water.
         6/ And that vessel was floating on the waters, but all the
         bulls and elephants and camels and asses sank to the bot-
         tom together with every animal, so that I could not see
         them. And they were unable to escape but perished and
         sank in the deep. 7/ And again I saw in the vision until
         those water channels were removed from that high roof
         and the fountains of the floor were stopped up, and other
         abysses were opened. 8/ And the water began to descend
         into them until the floor was uncovered and that vessel

---

  a Aram: Eth *those white bulls.*

  b Three mss read *without his trembling:* Aram omits the phrase.

  c Aram: Eth *a large ship,* perhaps an omission of adjective in Aram. See *1 Enoch 1,*
368.

  d Aram text in vv 2-8 is generally shorter than Eth, which is followed here because
it is complete and Aram is fragmentary. See *1 Enoch 1,* 368. Part of the difference seems
due to different cosmologies: the Aram a straightforward summary of Genesis; Eth,
depicting the cosmos as a great building with a courtyard (*enclosure*) set on earth. See
1 Enoch 1, 375–76.

settled onto the floor, and darkness withdrew and it became light.

From the Disembarkation to the Exodus

9   That white bull who had become a man came out of that vessel, and the three bulls with him. And one of those three bulls was white like that bull, and one of them was red like blood, and one of them was black. And that white bull departed from them. 10/ And they began to beget wild beasts and birds, so that there arose from them every kind of species: lions, leopards, wolves, dogs, hyenas, wild boars, foxes, conies, pigs, falcons, vultures, kites, eagles,[a] and ravens. But among them a white bull was born. 11/ And they began to bite one another, but that white bull that was born among them begot a wild ass and a white bull with it, and the wild asses increased. 12/ But that bull[b] that was born from it begot a black wild boar and a white ram of the flock. And that (wild boar) begot many boars, and that ram begat twelve sheep.

13   When those twelve sheep had grown up, they handed over one of themselves to the wild asses, and those wild asses, in turn, handed that sheep over to the wolves, and that sheep grew up among the wolves. 14/ And the ram led forth the eleven sheep to dwell with it and to pasture with it among the wolves. And they multiplied and became many flocks of sheep.

15   And the wolves began to fear them and oppress them until they did away with their young, and they cast their young into a river of much water. And those sheep began to cry out because of their young and to make complaint to their Lord. 16/ And a sheep that had escaped safely from the wolves fled and went off to the wild asses. And I saw the sheep groan-

---

a Identity of these species of birds is uncertain.
b Aram *calf.*

ing and crying out and petitioning their Lord with all their might, until that Lord of the sheep descended from a lofty chamber at the voice of the sheep, and he came to them and saw them. 17/ And he summoned that sheep that had fled from the wolves, and he spoke to it about the wolves, that it should testify against them not to touch the sheep. 18/ And the sheep went to the wolves at the command of the Lord, and another sheep met that sheep and went with it. And the two of them went and entered together into the assembly of those wolves. And they spoke to them and testified against them that they should not henceforth touch the sheep. 19/ After this I saw the wolves, how they dealt more harshly with the sheep with all their might, and (how) the sheep cried out. 20/ And their Lord came to the sheep and began to strike the wolves, and the wolves began to lament. But the sheep were quiet, and thereafter they did not cry out.

21   And I looked at the sheep until they went out from the wolves, and the wolves' eyes were blinded, and the wolves went out pursuing those sheep with all their might. 22/ And the Lord of the sheep went with them, leading them, and all his sheep followed him. And his face was dazzling and glorious and fearful to look at. 23/ And the wolves began to pursue those sheep until they met them by a swamp of water. 24/ And that swamp of water was split apart, and the water stood to one side and the other before them. And their Lord, as he led them, stood between them and the wolves. 25/ And as those wolves still did not see the sheep, they went into the midst of that swamp of water. The wolves pursued the sheep, and those wolves ran after them into that swamp of water. 26/ And when they saw the Lord of the sheep, they turned to flee from his presence, but that swamp of water flowed together and suddenly returned to its natural state. And the water swelled up and rose until it covered those wolves. 27/ And I saw until all the wolves that had pursued those sheep perished and sank.

From the Exodus to Moses' Death

28   But the sheep departed from that water and went out to a
       desert, where there was no water or grass, and they began to
       open their eyes and see. And I saw <until>[a] the Lord of the
       sheep was pasturing them and giving them water and grass,
       and that sheep was going and leading them. 29/ That sheep
       went up to the summit of a high rock, and the Lord of the
       sheep sent it to them. 30/ And after that, I saw the Lord of
       the sheep who stood before them, and his appearance was
       majestic and fearful and mighty, and all those sheep saw him
       and were afraid before him. 31/ And all of them were afraid
       and trembling because of him, and they were crying out
       after that sheep with the other sheep that was in their midst,
       'We cannot stand before our Lord or look at him.' 32/ And
       again that sheep that led them went up to the summit of
       that rock, and the sheep began to be blinded and to stray
       from the path that it had shown them, but the sheep did
       not know about these things. 33/ And the Lord of the sheep
       was filled with great wrath against them, and that sheep
       discovered it and went down from the summit of that rock
       and came to the sheep and found most of them blinded
       and straying. 34/ And when they saw it, they were afraid
       and trembled before it, and wished to return to their folds.
       35/ And that sheep took other sheep with it and went against
       those sheep that had strayed and began to slaughter them,
       and the sheep were afraid of it. And that sheep returned all
       the straying flock to their folds.[b]

36   And I saw in this vision, until that sheep became a man and
       built a house for the Lord of the sheep and made all the
       sheep stand in that house. 37/ And I saw until that sheep
       that had met that sheep that had led them fell asleep. And
       I saw until all the large sheep perished, and little ones arose
       in their place, and they came to a pasture and approached a

---

a Conjunction supplied, a cliché in this vision.

b Following the wording of Aram.

river of water. 38/ And that sheep that had led them, that had become a man, was separated from them and fell asleep, and all the sheep searched for him and cried bitterly because of him.

From the Entrance into the Land
to the Building of the Temple

39   And I saw until they ceased crying for that sheep and crossed that stream of water, and <two>[a] sheep arose that led them instead of those that had fallen asleep; and they led them. 40/ And I saw the sheep until they were entering a good place and a pleasant and glorious land. And I saw those sheep until they were satisfied, and that house was in their midst in the pleasant land.

41   And sometimes their eyes were opened, and sometimes they were blinded, until another sheep arose and led them and brought them all back, and their eyes were opened.

42   And the dogs began to devour the sheep, and the wild boars and the foxes were devouring them, until the Lord of the sheep raised up a ram from among the sheep, which led them.[b] 43/ And this ram began to butt and pursue with its horns. And it hurled itself against the foxes and, after them, against the wild boars; and it destroyed many wild boars. And after them it <struck> the dogs.[c] 44/ And the sheep whose eyes were open saw the ram among the sheep until it forsook its path and began to walk where there was no path.[d] 45/ And the Lord of the sheep sent this sheep to another sheep to appoint it to be ram, to rule the sheep instead of the ram that had forsaken its way. 46/ And it went to it and spoke with it secretly, alone, and appointed it to be ram and ruler and leader of the sheep. And during all these things,

---

a Eth corrupt.

b Translation follows mainly Gk fragment against corrupt Eth.

c Translation follows Gk, emending ērxato (*began*) to ēraxato (*struck*). See Tiller, *Commentary*, 369.

d Translation follows mainly Gk.

the dogs were oppressing the sheep. 47/ And the first ram pursued the second ram, and the second ram arose and fled before it. Then I looked at the first ram until it fell before the dogs.

48   And the second ram arose and led the sheep. **49/** And the sheep grew and multiplied, and all the dogs and foxes fled from it and feared it. And that ram butted and killed all the beasts, and those beasts did not prevail again among the sheep, nor did they snatch anything at all away from them. **48b/** And that ram begot many sheep, and it fell asleep.

And a little sheep became ram instead of it, and it became ruler and leader of those sheep. **50/** And that house became large and broad. And a large and high tower was built upon that house for the Lord of the sheep.[a] That house was low, but the tower was raised up and was high. And the Lord of the sheep stood on that tower, and they spread a full table before him.

The Apostasy of the Two Kingdoms

51   And again I saw that those sheep strayed and went off in many paths and abandoned that house of theirs. And the Lord of the sheep summoned some from among the sheep and sent them to the sheep, and the sheep began to kill them, 52/ but one of them escaped safely and was not killed. It sprang away and cried out over the sheep, and they wished to kill it; but the Lord of the sheep saved it from the hands of the sheep and brought it up to me and made it dwell (there). 53/ And many other sheep he sent to those sheep to testify and lament over them.

54   After that I saw when they abandoned the house of the Lord and his tower, they went astray in everything, and their eyes were blinded. And I saw that the Lord of the sheep worked

---

a For the textual confusion in this passage, see *1 Enoch 1*, 369–70; Tiller, *Commentary*, 312–13.

much slaughter on them in their pastures, <because>ᵃ those sheep invited that slaughter and betrayed his place. 55/ And he abandoned them into the hands of the lions and the leopards and the wolves and the hyenas and into the hands of the foxes and to all the beasts; and those wild beasts began to tear those sheep in pieces. 56/ And I saw that he abandoned that house of theirs and their tower, and he threw them all into the hands of the lions so that they might tear them in pieces and devour them—into the hands of all the beasts. 57/ And I began to cry out with all my might and to call to the Lord of the sheep and to show him concerning the sheep, because they were devoured by all the wild beasts. 58/ And he was silent, though he saw (it), and he rejoiced because they were devoured and swallowed up and carried off, and he abandoned them into the hands of all the beasts as fodder.

From the Destruction of Jerusalem to the End Time

The Commissioning of the Seventy Shepherds and the Angelic Scribe

59   And he summoned seventy shepherds, and he left those sheep to them, that they might pasture them. And he said to the shepherds and their subordinates, 'Every one of you from now on shall pasture the sheep, and everything that I command you, do. 60/ I am handing them over to you duly numbered, and I will tell you which of them are to be destroyed. Destroy them.' And he handed those sheep over to them.

61   And another one he summoned and said to him, 'Observe and see everything that the shepherds do against these sheep, for they will destroy more of them than I have commanded them. 62/ Every excess and destruction that is done by the

---

a Emending Eth ʾeska (*until*) to ʾesma (*because*).

shepherds, write down—how many they destroy at my command, and how many they destroy on their own. Every destruction by each individual shepherd, write down against them. 63/ And by number read them in my presence—how many they destroy and how many they hand over to destruction, so that I may have this testimony against them, that I may know every deed of the shepherds, that I may <measure>[a] them and see what they are doing—whether they are acting according to the command that I gave them or not. 64/ And do not let them know it, and do not show them or rebuke them. But write down every destruction by the shepherds, one by one, in his own time, and bring it all up to me.'

The First Period: The Twelve Shepherds until the Exile

65   And I saw until those shepherds were pasturing <each>[b] in his time, and they began to kill and destroy many more than they had been commanded, and they abandoned those sheep into the hands of the lions. 66/ And the lions and leopards devoured and swallowed up most of those sheep, and the wild boars devoured along with them, and they burnt down that tower and demolished that house. 67/ And I grieved exceedingly over that tower and because that house of the sheep had been demolished. And from then on I was unable to see whether those sheep were going into that house.

68   And the shepherds and their subordinates handed over those sheep to all the wild beasts, to devour them. And each of them, individually, in his time, was given over by number, and by number each of them handed over[c] to his companion. In a book it was written[d] how many of them he was

---

a Conjecture: Eth corrupt.

b Slight Eth emendation.

c Clause omitted in most mss, perhaps due to its similarity to the previous one.

d Verb forms vary in mss.

destroying. 69/ And more than was prescribed for them each of them was killing and destroying, and I began to weep and lament because of those sheep. 70/ And thus in the vision I saw how that one who was writing was writing down each one that was being destroyed by those shepherds every day, and (how) he was bringing up and <spreading out>[a] and showing that whole book to the Lord of the sheep, everything that they had done, and everything that each one of them had taken away, and everything that they had handed over to destruction. 71/ And the book was read in the presence of the Lord of the sheep, and he took the book from his hand and read it and set it down. 72a/ <And I saw until>[b] the shepherds were pasturing for twelve hours.

The Second Period: the Twenty-three Shepherds from the Return to Alexander

72b   And look, three of those sheep returned and came and entered and began to build all that had fallen down from that house. And the wild boars tried to hinder them, but they could not. 73/ And they began again to build as before and they raised up that tower and it was called the high tower. And they began again to place a table before the tower, but all the bread on it was polluted and not pure. 74/ And besides all these things, the eyes of the sheep were blind, and they did not see, and their shepherds likewise. And they handed them over to <the wild beasts>[c] for greater destruction, and they trampled the sheep with their feet and devoured them. 75/ And the Lord of the sheep remained silent until all the sheep were scattered over the field and were mixed with them, and they did not save them from the hand of the beasts. 76/ And this one who was writing the

---

a Emending Gk *anepause* (*causing to rest*) to *aneptusse*. See Tiller, *Commentary*, 330.

b Text *And after that I saw the shepherds pasturing for twelve hours.* On the emendation, see *1 Enoch 1*, 389, 392–93.

c Text *the shepherds*, a dittograph from previous line.

book brought it up and showed it and read it in the houses[a] of the Lord of the sheep. And he interceded with him in their behalf and petitioned him in their behalf, showing him every deed of the shepherds, and he testified in his presence against all the shepherds. 77/ And he took the book and set it down by him and went out.

90:1 And I saw until the time when <thirty-five>[b] shepherds had been pasturing in this manner, and they all completed their respective times like the first ones. And others received them into their hands to pasture them in their respective times, each shepherd in his time.

The Third Period: the Twenty-three Shepherds from Alexander into the Second Century

2 After this in my vision I saw all the birds of heaven come— eagles and vultures and kites and ravens, and the eagles were leading all the birds. And they began to devour those sheep and peck out their eyes and devour their flesh. 3/ And the sheep cried out because their flesh was being devoured by the birds, and I cried out and lamented in my sleep because of that shepherd who was pasturing the sheep. 4/ And I saw until those sheep were devoured by the dogs and by the eagles and by the kites. And they left them neither flesh nor skin nor sinew, until only their bones remained; and their bones fell on the earth, and the sheep became few. 5/ And I saw until the time that twenty-three shepherds had been pasturing, and they completed in their respective times fifty-eight times.

---

a On the textual problem, see Tiller, *Commentary*, 342. On the plural *houses*, cf. 14:10-15.

b Text *thirty-seven*.

The Fourth Period: the Twelve Shepherds
Until the End Time

6   And look, lambs were born of those white sheep, and they
         began to open their eyes and to see and to cry out to the
         sheep. 7/ But they did not listen to them[a] nor attend to their
         words, but they were extremely deaf, and their eyes were
         extremely and excessively blinded. 8/ And I saw in the vision
         that the ravens flew upon those lambs and seized one of those
         lambs[b] and dashed the sheep in pieces and devoured them.
         9/ And I saw until horns came out on those lambs, and the
         ravens were casting down their horns. {*And I saw until a great
         horn sprouted on one of those sheep. 10/ And it looked on them,
         and their eyes were opened, and it cried out to the sheep, and
         the rams saw it, and they all ran to it.*}11/ And besides this, all
         those eagles and vultures and ravens and kites were still tear-
         ing the sheep in pieces and flying upon them and devouring
         them. And the sheep were silent, but the rams lamented and
         cried out.[c] {*12/ And those ravens were struggling and fighting
         with it and wished to do away with its horn, but they did not
         prevail against it. 13/ And I saw until the shepherds and the
         eagles and those vultures and the kites came, and they cried to
         the ravens to smash the horn of that ram, and they struggled and
         made war with it, and it was struggling with them and cried out
         that its help might come. 14/ And I looked until that man came
         who wrote the names of the shepherds and brought (them) before
         the Lord of the sheep and he helped it and showed it everything;
         his help came down to that ram. 15/ And I saw until the Lord of
         the sheep came upon them in wrath, and all that saw him fled
         and all fell into darkness[d] before him. 16/ And all the eagles and
         vultures and ravens and kites gathered and brought with them*}

---

a Mss read a variety of verbs. See *1 Enoch 1*, 389.

b On the textual problem, see Tiller, *Commentary*, 352–53.

c Italicized verses (9b-10, 12-16), which describe the activity of Judas Maccabeus,
appear to be a doublet of vv 6-9a, 11, 17-19. If so, they are an update of a slightly earlier
apocalypse, interpolated around 163–161 B.C.E.

d Oldest Eth ms: others read (*his*) *shadow.*

all the wild <beasts>,[a] *and they all came together and helped one another smash the horn of that ram.}* 17/ And I looked at that man who wrote the book at the word of the Lord, until he opened the book of the destruction that those last twelve shepherds worked, and he showed before the Lord of the sheep that they had destroyed more than those before them. 18/ And I saw until the Lord of the sheep came to them and took in his hand the staff of his wrath and struck the earth, and the earth was split, and all the beasts and all the birds of heaven fell (away) from among those sheep and sank in the earth, and it covered over them. 19/ And I saw until a large sword was given to those sheep, and the sheep went out against all the wild beasts to kill them, and all the beasts and the birds of heaven fled before them.

The Judgment and the New Age

The Judgment

20   And I saw until a throne was constructed in the pleasant land and the Lord of the sheep sat upon it, and he took all the sealed books and opened those books before the Lord of the sheep. 21/ And the Lord summoned those first seven white men, and he commanded them to bring before him beginning with the first star that had preceded those stars whose organs were like the organs of horses,[b] and they brought all of them before him. 22/ And he said to the man who had been writing before him—who was one of those seven white ones—he said to him, 'Bring those seventy shepherds to whom I delivered the sheep and who took and killed more than I commanded them.' 23/ And look, I saw all of them bound, and they all stood before him. 24/ And judgment was exacted first on the stars, and they were judged and found to be sinners. And they went to the place of judgment, and they threw them into an abyss; and it was full of fire, and it was burning and was full of

---

a Emended from *wild sheep*, which have not been previously mentioned.
b A few evidently superfluous words have been dropped here. See *1 Enoch 1*, 403.

pillars of fire. 25/ And those seventy shepherds were judged and found to be sinners, and they were thrown into that fiery abyss. 26/ And I saw at that time that an abyss like it was opened in the middle of the earth, which was full of fire. And they brought those blinded sheep, and they were all judged and found to be sinners. And they were thrown into that fiery abyss, and they burned. And that abyss was to the south of that house. 27/ And I saw those sheep burning and their bones burning.

A New Beginning

28   And I stood up to see, until that old house was folded up[a]— and they removed all the pillars, and all the beams and ornaments of that house were folded up with it—and they removed it and put it in a place to the south of the land. 29/ And I saw until the Lord of the sheep brought a new house, larger and higher than that first one, and he erected it on the site of the first one that had been rolled up. And all its pillars were new, and its beams were new, and its ornaments were new and larger than (those of) the first one, the old one that he had removed. And all the sheep were within it.

30   And I saw all the sheep that remained. And all the animals on the earth and all the birds of heaven were falling down and worshiping those sheep and making petition to them and obeying them in every thing.[b]

31   After that, those three who were clothed in white and who had taken hold of me by my hand, who had previously brought me up (with the hand of that ram also taking hold of me), set me down among those sheep before the judgment took place.

32   And all those sheep were white, and their wool was thick and pure. 33/ And all that had been destroyed and dispersed <by>[c] all the wild beasts and all the birds of heaven were

---

a Some witnesses read *submerged*, evidently an Eth corruption.

b Lit. *Every word*, reflecting Aram *millaʾ*, which can mean *word* or *thing*.

c Emended from *and*.

gathered in that house. And the Lord of the sheep rejoiced greatly because they were all good and had returned to that house. 34/ And I saw until they laid down that sword that had been given to the sheep; they brought it back to his house and sealed it up in the presence of the Lord. And all the sheep were enclosed in that house, but it did not contain them. 35/ And the eyes of all were opened, and they saw good things; and there was none among them that did not see. 36/ And I saw how that house was large and broad and very full.

37   And I saw how a white bull was born, and its horns were large. And all the wild beasts and all the birds of heaven were afraid of it and made petition to it continually. 38/ And I saw until all their species were changed, and they all became white cattle. And the first one became <leader>[a] among them (and that <leader> was a large animal), and there were large black horns on its head. And the Lord of the sheep rejoiced over it and over all the cattle.

The Conclusion to the Vision

39   And I slept among them and awoke. And I saw everything, 40/ and this is the vision that I saw while I slept. And I awoke and blessed the Lord of righteousness and gave him glory. 41/ And after that I wept bitterly, and my tears did not cease until I could no longer endure it, but they were running down because of what I had seen; for everything will come to pass and be fulfilled, and every deed of humanity was shown to me in its order. 42/ That night I remembered the first dream. I wept because of it, and I was disturbed because I had seen the vision."

---

a Text reads *word*. A major crux of interpretation. For the various suggested emendations, see *1 Enoch 1*, 403.

A Narrative Bridge

(Chapter 91:1-9, 18-19)

91:1 And now, my son Methuselah,
  Call to me all your brothers,
    and gather to me all the children of your mother.
  For a voice is calling me,
    and a spirit is poured out upon me,
      so that I may show you everything that will happen to you
      forever.

2 Then Methuselah went and called all his brothers to him and
    gathered his relatives.

3 And he spoke (of) righteousness to all his sons,[a] and he said:
  "Hear, O sons of Enoch, every word of your father,
    and listen aright to the voice of my mouth;
      for I testify to you and speak to you, my beloved.

4 Love the truth and walk in it;
    but do not draw near to the truth with a double heart,
    and do not associate with those of a double heart.
  But walk in righteousness, my children;
    and it will guide you in the paths of goodness,
    and righteousness will be your companion.

5 For I know that the state of violence will grow strong on the
    earth,

  and a great scourge will be consummated on the earth.
  Indeed, all iniquity will be consummated,
    but it will be cut off from its roots,
    and its whole structure will vanish.

---

a Eth mss vary in their wording of this clause.

6   And again iniquity will be consummated on the earth,
              and all the deeds of iniquity and violence and sin will
                  prevail again.
7   And when sin and iniquity and blasphemy and violence
                  increase in every deed,
              and perversity and sin and uncleanness increase,
          a great scourge will come from heaven upon all these,
              and the holy Lord will come forth in wrath and with a
                  scourge,
              to execute judgment upon the earth.
8   And in those days, violence will be cut off from its roots,
              as well as the roots of iniquity, together with deceit,
              and they will be destroyed from under heaven.
9   And all the idols of the nations will be given up,
              and the tower(s) will be burned with fire.
          They will be removed from all the earth,
              and they will be thrown into the fiery judgment,
              and they will be destroyed in fierce, everlasting judgment.
10   {And the righteous will arise from his sleep,
              and wisdom will arise and be given to them.}[a]
11–17   . . . .
18   And now I tell you, my children,
              and I show you the paths of righteousness and the paths of
                  violence,
              and I shall show you[b] them again, that you may know
                  what is coming.
19   And now hear me, my children,
              and walk in the paths of righteousness,
              and do not walk in the paths of violence;
          for they will perish forever—
              all who walk in the paths of iniquity."[c]

---

a Verses 10-17 are textually problematic. Vv 11-17 have been displaced from their
original location after 93:10 (where they are relocated in this translation). V 10 appears
to have been created to provide a transition when vv 11-17 were moved here. Additionally, Aram has textual material here with no counterpart in Eth. See *1 Enoch 1*, 413–15.
   b Three mss read *and I have shown you.*
   c Fragmentary Aram indicates a longer and different form of these two lines.

The Epistle of Enoch

(Chapters 92–105)

Introduction (Chapter 92)

92:1   Written by Enoch the scribe (this complete sign of wisdom)ᵃ (who is) praised by all people and a leader of the whole earth, to all my sons who will dwell on the earth, and to the last generations who will observe truth and peace.

2   Let not your spirit be troubled because of the times;
for the Great Holy One has appointed days for everything.

3   The righteous one will arise from sleep;
he will arise and walk in the paths of righteousness,
and all his path and his journey (will be) in piety and
everlasting mercy.

4   And (God) will be merciful to the righteous one,
and to him he will give everlasting truth;
and (to him) he will give authority,
and he will judgeᵇ in piety and in righteousness;
and he will walk in everlasting light.

5   Sin will be destroyed in darkness forever;
and it will not be seen from that day forever.

---

a Somewhat different fragmentary Aram here and in v 2 cannot be reconstructed with certainty.

b Eth: *wayekwēnnen*. Many mss read *wayekawwen* (*and he will be*).

The Apocalypse of Weeks (93:1-10; 91:11-17)

Introduction

93:1   After this Enoch took up his discourse^a, saying,
2   "Concerning the sons of righteousness,
      and concerning the chosen of eternity,
      and concerning the plant of truth,
   these things I say to you
      and I make known to you, my sons,
      I myself, Enoch.
   The vision of heaven was shown to me,
      and from the words of the watchers and holy ones I have
         learned everything,
      and in the heavenly tablets I read everything and I
         understood."^b

The Apocalypse

3   And Enoch took up his discourse and said,
   "I was born the seventh in the first week,
      and until my time righteousness endured.
4   After me there will arise a second week,
      in which deceit and violence will spring up,
      and in it will be the first end,
      and in it a man will be saved.
   And after <that, at its conclusion>,^c iniquity will increase,
      and a law will be made for sinners.

---

a Lit. *parable*; cf.1:2. Translation follows reconstructed Aram. Eth or its Gk corrupt. See *1 Enoch 1*, 435.

b Aram and Eth of these two lines differ. Original wording uncertain. See *1 Enoch 1*, 435.

c Eth *after it is completed*. Emended by analogy with Eth 93:5, 6, 7, 8, 10; 91:13.

5   After this <there will arise a third week,
             and at its conclusion>ᵃ a man will be chosen as the plant
                 of righteous judgment,
             and after him will go forth the plant of righteousness
                 forever and ever.
6   After this <there will arise a fourth week,
             and at its conclusion>, visions of the holy and righteous
                 will be seen,
             and a covenant for all generations and a tabernacle will be
                 made in it.ᵇ
7   After this <there will arise a fifth week
             and at its conclusion>, <the temple of the glorious
                 kingdom>ᶜ will be built forever.
8   After this <there will arise a sixth week,
             and> all who live in it will become blind,
             and the hearts of all will stray from wisdom;
             and in it a man will ascend.
         And at its conclusion,ᵈ the temple of the kingdom will be
                 burned with fire,
             and in it the whole race of the chosen root will be
                 dispersed.
9   After this, in the seventh week, there will arise a perverse
                 generation,
             and many will be its deeds,
             and all its deeds will be perverse.
10   And at its conclusion, the chosen will be chosen,
             as witnesses of righteousnessᵉ from the everlasting plant of
                 righteousness,
             to whom will be given sevenfold wisdom and knowledge.ᶠ

---

    a Verb *arise* supplied in 93:5, 6, 7, 8 by analogy with Aram Eth v 4 and Eth v 9.
See *1 Enoch 1*, 436.
    b Copt: Eth *for them.*
    c Eth *the house of glory and kingdom.* Translation imitates Aram 91:13.
    d Eth *at the close of the week.*
    e Phrase from Aram: Eth omits.
    f Phrase from Aram: Eth *sevenfold wisdom concerning all his creation,* reflecting
verse's juxtaposition with 93:11 in all mss.

91:11   And they will uproot the foundations of violence,
              and the structure of deceit in it,
              to execute judgment.[a]

12   After this there will arise an eighth week of righteousness,
              in which a sword will be given to all the righteous,
              to execute righteous judgment on all the wicked,
              and they will be delivered into their hands.

13   And at its conclusion, they will acquire possessions[b] in
                  righteousness,
              and the temple of the kingdom of the Great One will be
                  built in the greatness of its glory
              for all the generations of eternity.[c]

14   After this there will arise a ninth week,
              in which righteous law will be revealed to all the sons of
                  the whole earth,
              and all the deeds[d] of wickedness will vanish from the
                  whole earth and descend to the everlasting pit,[e]
              and all humankind will look to the path of everlasting
                  righteousness.

15   After this, in the tenth week, the seventh part, (will be) the
                  everlasting judgment,
              and it will be executed on the watchers of the eternal
                  heaven,
              <and a fixed time of the great judgment will be rendered
                  among the holy ones>.[f]

16   And the first heaven will pass away in it,
              and a new heaven will appear,
              and all the powers of the heavens will shine forever with
                  sevenfold (brightness).[g]

---

a Translation follows Aram: Eth much longer, has been modified to fit its new
place after 91:10. See *1 Enoch 1*, 436.

b Aram: Eth *houses*.

c Aram: Eth *forever*.

d Or perhaps *doers*.

e Reconstructed Aram: Eth corrupt. See *1 Enoch 1*, 437.

f On the complex textual witnesses to this verse, see *1 Enoch 1*, 437.

g Exact wording of this line and v 17b uncertain. See *1 Enoch 1*, 437.

17   After this there will be many weeks without number forever,
            in which they will do piety and righteousness,
            and from then on sin will never again be mentioned."

Enoch Recapitulates His Revelation: A Fragment (93:11-14)

93:11   . . . . .ᵃ
            For who is there of all the sons of men who is able to hear the
                words[b] of the Holy One and not be terrified;
            and who is able to think his thoughts?
            And who is there of all men[c] who is able to look at all the
                works of heaven,[d]
12   . . . . ?
            Or to see a soul or a spirit
                and is able to tell?[e]
            Or to ascend and see all their ends,
                and to consider them or make (something) like them?
13   Or who is there of all men who is able to know what is the
                width and length of the earth;[f]
            and to whom has the size of all[g] them been shown?
14   And who is there of all men who is able to know the length
                of the heavens,
            and what is their height and upon what they are founded?
            And what is the number of the stars,
                and where all the luminaries rest?[h]

---

   a This section is attested in Aram in a somewhat fuller, albeit fragmentary form,
which indicates at least one line before v 11a. See *1 Enoch 1*, 451.

   b Aram: Eth *word* or *voice*.

   c Eth omits *of all men*.

   d Text of this unit is uncertain. Eth has two lines that are evident doublets of the
previous one. See *1 Enoch 1*, 451.

   e Aram *or return to* [*tell*].

   f Aram *the length and width of the whole earth*.

   g Aram adds *and its shape*.

   h Aram appears not to have had this line.

Enoch's Instruction on the Two Ways (94:1-5)

94:1   And now I say to you, my children:
       Love righteousness and walk in it;
              for the paths of righteousness are worthy of acceptance,
              but the paths of iniquity will quickly be destroyed and
                 vanish.
2   And to certain people of a generation the paths of violence
                 and death will be revealed;
              and they will keep away from them,
              and they will not follow them.
3   And now I say to you, O righteous:
       Walk not in the paths of evil, nor in the paths of death;
              approach them not, lest you be destroyed.
4   But seek and choose for yourselves righteousness and an elect
                 life;
              and walk in the paths of peace,
              that you may live and prosper.
5   Hold fast the thought of your heart,
              and do not erase my word from your heart.
       For I know that sinners will tempt people to do harm to
                 wisdom;
              and no place will be found for her,
              and none of the temptation will diminish.

Enoch's First Discourse:
Social Oppression (94:6—96:3)

Woes Against the Violent and Rich

6   Woe to those who build iniquity and violence,
              and lay deceit as a foundation;
                 for quickly they will be overthrown,
                 and they will have no peace.
7   Woe to those who build their houses with sin;
                 for from all their foundations they will be overthrown,
                 and by the sword they will fall.

And those who acquire gold and silver in judgment will
   quickly perish.

8   Woe to you, rich, for in your riches you have trusted;
         from your riches you will depart,
            because you have not remembered the Most High in the
               days of your riches.

9   You have committed blasphemy and iniquity;
         and you have been prepared for the day of bloodshed
         and the day of darkness and the day of great judgment.

10   Thus I say and make known to you:
      He who created you will overturn you;
         and for your fall there will be no compassion,
         and your Creator will rejoice at your destruction.

11   And your righteous ones in those days will be a reproach to
         the sinners and the wicked.

95:1 O that my eyes were a <fountain>[a] of water,
         that I might weep over you;
      I would pour out my tears as a cloud of water,
         and I would rest from the grief of my heart.

2   Who has permitted you to practice hatred and evil?
      The judgment will overtake you,[b] sinners.

An Exhortation to the Righteous

3   Fear not the sinners, O righteous;
         for the Lord will again deliver them into your hand,
            that you may execute judgment on them as you desire.

A Second String of Woes

4   Woe to you who utter anathemas that you cannot loose;[c]
         healing will be far from you on account of your sins.

5   Woe to you who repay your neighbor with evil;
         for you will be repaid according to your deeds.

---

a Presuming an Aram corruption from ʿayn to ʿanan (cloud, Eth mss).
b Lit. will find you.
c Some mss read cannot be loosed and can be loosed.

6   Woe to you, lying witnesses, and those who weigh out
            injustice;
        for quickly you will be destroyed.
7   Woe to you sinners because you persecute the righteous;
            for you will be handed over and persecuted because of
                injustice,
        and their yoke[a] will be heavy upon you.

Two More Exhortations

96:1   Be hopeful, O righteous;
            for quickly the sinners will perish before you,
            and you will have authority over them as you desire.
2   On the day of the tribulation of the sinners,
        your children will mount up and ascend like eagles,
            and higher than the vultures will be your nest;
        you will climb up and enter the crevices of the earth,
            and the clefts of the rock forever,
            like conies, before the lawless.
        And they will sigh because of you
            and weep like[b] sirens.
3   Fear not, you who have suffered;
            for you will receive healing,
            and a bright light will shine upon you,
            and the voice of rest you will hear from heaven.

Enoch's Second Discourse: The Abuses of Wealth and the Judgment of the Rich (96:4—98:8)

Woes Against the Rich

96:4   Woe to you, sinners, for your riches make you appear to be
            righteous,
            but your heart convicts you of being sinners;
        and this word will be a testimony against you,
            a reminder of (your) evil deeds.

---

a Some mss read *its yoke*.

b Two mss omit *like*, making *sirens* the subject of the verb.

5   Woe to you who devour the finest of the wheat,
            and quaff <wine from the mixing bowl>,ᵃ
            while you tread on the lowly with your might.
6   Woe to you who drink water <from every fountain>;ᵇ
            for quickly you will be repaid, and cease and dry up,
            because you have forsaken the fountain of life.
7   Woe to you who commit iniquity and deceit and blasphemy;
            it will be a reminder against you for evil.
8   Woe to you, mighty, who with might oppress the righteous
            one;
            for the day of your destruction will come.
        In those days, many good days will come for the righteous
        —in the day of your judgment.

An Exhortation to the Righteous

97:1   <Take courage,>ᶜ O righteous;
            for the sinners will become an object of contempt,
            and they will be destroyed on the day of iniquity.
2   Be it known to you that the Most High has your destruction
            in mind,
            and the angels of heaven <make disclosure>ᵈ concerning
            your destruction.

To the Sinners: On the Judgment

3   And what will you do, O sinners,
            and where will you flee on that day of judgment,
            when you hear the words of the prayer of the righteous?

---

    a Eth *drink the strength of the root of the fountain* is corrupt. Emendation based on
Amos 6:6 and posits corruptions in Aram and the Gk behind the Eth. See *1 Enoch 1*,
468.
    b Eth *all the time.* Aram corruption emended to fit v 6c. See *1 Enoch 1*, 468.
    c Eth *have faith*, a normal translation of *take courage* in Eth NT. Cf. below 102:4;
104:2.
    d Eth *rejoice.* Presuming Aram corruption. See *1 Enoch 1, 468.*

4   You will not[a] be like them;
        for this word will be a testimony against you:
        "†You have been companions of sinners.†"[b]
5   In those days, the prayer of the righteous will come to the
        Lord;
        but to you the days of your judgment will come.
6   And all the words of your lawless deeds will be read out
        before the Great Holy One,
        and your face will be <put to shame>;[c]
        then he will remove all the deeds that partook[d] in
        lawlessness.

Woes Against the Rich

7   Woe to you, sinners, who are in the midst of the sea and on
        the land;
        the reminder against you is evil.
8   Woe to you who acquire gold and silver unjustly and say,
        "We have become very wealthy,
        and we have gotten possessions,
        and we have acquired all that we have wished.
9   And now let us do what we have wished,[e]
        for silver we have gathered up in our treasuries,
        and many goods in our houses;
        and as water they are poured out."
10   You err!
        For your wealth will not remain,
        but will quickly ascend from you;
        for you have acquired everything unjustly,
        and you will be delivered to a great curse.

---

a Four Eth mss omit *not*.
b For possible corruption, see *1 Enoch 1*, 473.
c Eth *received*: Gk slightly corrupt. See *1 Enoch 1*, 469.
d Gk: Eth *were founded in*.
e Gk defective here. For textual problems, see *1 Enoch 1*, 469.

An Oath to the Wise

98:1   And now I swear to you, the wise, and not the foolish,
             that you will see many (things) on the earth.
2   For men will put on adornments as women,
             and fair colors more than virgins,
             in kingship and majesty and power.
         And silver and gold will be among them as food,
             and in their houses these will be poured out like water,
3   because they have no knowledge or understanding.
         Thus they will perish, together with all their possessions,
             and all their splendor and honor;
         and for dishonor and slaughter and great destitution,
             their spirits will be cast into the fiery furnace.

Two Oaths to the Sinners: On Responsibility
and the Judgment

4   I swear to you, sinners,[a]
             that it was not ordained <for a man> to be a slave,
                 nor was <a decree> given for a woman to be a handmaid;
             but it happened because of oppression.
         Thus lawlessness was not sent upon the earth;
             but men created it by themselves,
             and those who do it will come to a great curse.
5   Likewise, neither is a woman created barren,
             but because of the works of her hands she is disgraced
                 with childlessness.
6   I swear to you, sinners, by the Great Holy One,
             that all your evil deeds are revealed in heaven,
             and you will have no unrighteous deed that is hidden.

---

    a Textual problems in vv 4-5 are complex. Eth speaks of *a mountain* becoming a
slave and *a hill* a handmaid. A double Gk text reflecting two different readings of Aram
suggests this is corrupt. See *1 Enoch 1*, 469–70.

7   Do not suppose to yourself nor say in your heart,
            that they do not know and your unrighteous deeds are not
                seen in heaven,
            nor are they written down before the Most High.
8   Henceforth know
            that all your unrighteous deeds are written down day by
                day
            until the day of your judgment.

Enoch's Third Discourse: True and False Religion and Their Consequences (98:9—99:10)

Woes Against Those Who Err

9   Woe to you, fools;
            for you will be destroyed because of your folly.
        You do not listen to the wise;
            and good things will not happen to you,
            but evils will surround you.
10   And now know that you have been prepared for a day of
                destruction,
            and do not hope to be saved, O sinners;
            you will depart and die.
        <Know> that you have been prepared for a day of great judg-
                ment and tribulation[a]
            and very great shame for your spirits.
11   Woe to you, stiff-necked and hard of heart,[b]
            who do evil and consume blood.
        From where do you have good things to eat and drink and be
                satisfied?
            From all the good things that the Lord, the Most High,
                has abundantly provided upon the earth.
            You will have no peace!

---

a For the textual problems in this line, see *1 Enoch 1*, 482.

b Eth omits *stiff-necked and*: Gk restored in lacuna. See *1 Enoch 1*, 482, 485.

12   Woe to you who love the deeds of iniquity;
            why do you have good hopes for yourselves?[a]
        Now be it known to you that you will be delivered into the
            hands of the righteous,
            and they will cut off your necks,
            and they will kill you and not spare you.
13   Woe to you who rejoice over the troubles of the righteous;
            your grave will not be dug.
14   Woe to you who annul the words of the righteous;
            you will have no hope of salvation.
15   Woe to those who write lying words and words of error;
            they write and lead many astray with their lies <when they
            hear them.>[b]
        You yourselves err;
16   you will have no peace but will quickly perish.
99:1   Woe to you who commit erring acts,
            and who for false deeds receive honor and glory;
            you will perish, you will have no salvation for good.
2   Woe to you who alter the true words
            and pervert the everlasting covenant
            and consider themselves to be without sin;
            they will be swallowed up in the earth.

The Righteous Encouraged to Pray for Judgment

3   Then be prepared, O righteous, and present your petitions as
            a reminder;
            offer them as a testimony before the angels,
            that they may bring in the sins of the unrighteous before
            the Most High as a reminder.
4   Then the nations will be thrown into confusion,
            and the families of the nations will be unsettled,
            on the day of the destruction of iniquity.

_____

    a *good hopes*, a typical Greek idiom that is perhaps the wording of the translator
rather than the author. See *1 Enoch 1*, 485–86.
    b Gk and Eth defective, but restorable. See *1 Enoch 1*, 482.

5   At that very time, those who are giving birth will bring forth,
            and they will <sell>ᵃ and abandon their young infant;
            and those who are with child will <abort>;ᵇ
        And those who are nursing will cast off their children,
            and they will not return to their infants or to their
                sucklings
        nor will they spare their beloved ones.

Another Warning to Those Who Err

6   Again I swear to you, sinners,
            that sin is prepared for a day of ceaseless bloodshed.
7   Those who worship stones—ᶜ
        and who carve images of silver and gold and wood and stone
                and clay
            and worship phantoms and demons and abomina-
                tions and evil spirits and all errors, not according to
                knowledge;
            no help will you find from them.
8   They will be led astray by the folly of their hearts,
            and their eyes will be blinded by the fear of their hearts,
            and the visions of (your) dreams will lead you astray—
9   You and the false works that you have made and constructed
                of stone,
            you will be destroyed together.

A Beatitude on Those Who Listen to the Wise

10   Then blessed will be all who listen to the words of the wise,
            and learn to do the commandments of the Most High;
        and walk in the paths of his righteousness,
            and do not err with the erring;
        for they will be saved.

---

a Gk Eth corrupt. See *1 Enoch 1*, 483.

b Gk defective: Eth corrupt, but restorable. See *1 Enoch 1*, 483.

c Translation of vv 7-9 reflects Gk, Eth, and Tertullian's Latin. See *1 Enoch 1*, 483.

Enoch's Fourth Discourse: A Stern Warning to the Sinners (99:11—100:6)

A Series of Woes

11   Woe to you who spread evil for your neighbor;
           for in Sheol you will be slain.
12   Woe to you who lay the foundations of sin and deceit,
           and cause bitterness on the earth;
           for because of it they will be brought to an end.
13   Woe to those who build their houses not with their own
              labors,
           and make the whole house of the stones and bricks of sin.[a]
        Woe to you; you will have no peace.
14   Woe to those who reject the foundation and everlasting
              inheritance of their fathers;
           and a spirit of error pursues you;[b]
        You will have no rest.
15   Woe to you who practice lawlessness and aid iniquity,
           murdering their neighbor until the day of the great
              judgment.
16   For he will destroy your glory and lay affliction on your
              hearts,
           and arouse his wrath against you,[c]
           and destroy all of you with the sword;
        But all the righteous and holy[d] will remember your
              unrighteous deeds.

A Description of the Judgment

100:1   And then in one place the fathers will be smitten with their
              sons,
           and brothers will fall in death with one another,
2e   From dawn until sunset they will be murdered together,[e]
1c   until there flows of their blood as it were a stream.

---

   a Text of this line uncertain. See *1 Enoch 1*, 495.
   b Gk: Eth variants make (*spirit of*) error object of the verb.
   c Gk defective. Precise wording uncertain.
   d Eth, also with reverse word order: Gk omits *and holy*. Cf. v 5.
   e Line moved to create a series of distichs. See *1 Enoch 1*, 499–500.

2   For a man will not restrain his hand from his son,
          nor from his beloved one, to kill him;
      and the sinner will not restrain his hand[a] from the honored
          one,
          nor from his brother.

3   A horse will wade up to its breast through the blood of the
          sinners,
          and the chariot will sink to its axles.

4   The angels will descend, going down into the hidden places
          on that day;
      and those who aided iniquity will be gathered into one
          place.[b]
      And the Most High will be aroused on that day[c]
          to execute great judgment on all.[d]

A Blessed Future

5   He will set a guard of the holy angels over all the righteous
          and holy;
      and they will be kept as the apple of the eye
      until evil and sin come to an end.
      And from that time,[e] the pious[f] will sleep a sweet sleep,
          and there will no longer[g] be anyone to frighten them.

6   And the wise among men will see the truth,[h]
      and the sons of the earth will contemplate these words[i] of
          this epistle,
      and they will recognize that their wealth cannot save them
          when iniquity collapses.

---

a Gk omits *will not restrain his hand.*

b On these two lines, see *1 Enoch 1*, 496.

c Gk and some Eth mss specify it as a day *of judgment.*

d Eth adds *the sinners*, perhaps a gloss.

e Gk: for Eth variants, see *1 Enoch 1*, 496.

f Gk: Eth *the righteous.*

g Eth *not.*

h Emending defective Gk after some Eth mss. See *1 Enoch 1*, 496.

i Eth *all the words.*

Enoch's Fifth Discourse: To the Sinners, on their Judgment (100:7—102:3)

A String of Woes

7   Woe to you, unrighteous,
> when you afflict the righteous on a day of hard anguish,
>> and burn them in fire;
> for you will be recompensed according to your deeds.

8   Woe to you, hard of heart,
> who lie awake to devise evil;
> fear will overtake you, and there will be no one to help
>> you.

9   Woe to you, all you sinners,
> because of the words of your mouth and the deeds of your
>> hands,
> for you have strayed from the holy deeds;
> in the heat of a blazing fire you will burn.

God Will Judge by Means of the Creation

10   And now know that from the angels inquiry into your deeds
>> will be made in heaven,
> and from the sun and from the moon and from the stars,
>> concerning your sins;
> because on earth you execute judgment on the righteous.

11   And every cloud and mist and dew and rain will testify
>> against you;
> for they will all be withheld from you, so as not to descend
>> upon you,[a]
> and they will be mindful of your sins.

12   Therefore, give gifts to the rain, lest it be withheld from
>> descending to you,
> and to the dew and clouds and mist pay gold, that they
>> may descend.

---

a Gk is defective here.

13   For if the snow and the frost and its cold hurl themselves
          upon you,
          and the winds and their chill and all their scourges,
          then[a] you will not be able to endure before the cold and
              their scourges.

An Appeal to the Evidence of Such a Judgment

101:1   So contemplate, O human beings,[b] the deeds of the Most
          High[c]
          and fear to do evil in his presence.
2   If he closes the windows of heaven,
          and withholds the dew and the rain from descending
              because of you,
          what will you do?
3   If he sends forth his wrath against you and your deeds,
          will you not be entreating him?
      Why do you speak with your mouth[d] proud and hard things
          against his majesty?
      You will have no peace.
4   Look at the captains who sail the sea!
      Their ships are shaken by wave and storm.
5   Being beaten by the storm, they all fear,
          and all their goods and possessions they throw out into the
              sea.[e]
      And in their heart they are apprehensive
          that the sea will swallow them up, and they will perish in
              it.
6   Are not all the sea and all its waters and all its movement the
          work of the Most High?

---

a Eth *in those days*, which normally translates *then* of Gk, missing here.

b Lit. *sons of men.*

c Eth line corrupt.

d Eth omits phrase. But cf. 5:4; 27:2.

e Gk and Eth of these two lines differ somewhat. Exact original wording uncertain.

He constituted it from the waters,
and bound it together and confined it by the sand.[a]

7   At his rebuke they fear and dry up,
and the fish die and all that is in it;
but you sinners on the earth do not fear him.

8   Did he not make the heavens and the earth and all that is in
them?
And who gave knowledge and wisdom to all that move on
the earth and that are in the sea?

9   Do not the captains fear the sea?
But the sinners do not fear the Most High.

The Final Enactment of Such Judgment

102:1   Then, when he hurls against you the flood of the fire of your
burning,
where will you flee and be saved?[b]
And when he utters his voice against you with a mighty
sound,
will you not be shaken and frightened?

2   The heavens and all the luminaries will be shaken with great
fear;
and all the earth will be shaken and will tremble and be
thrown into confusion.

3   All the angels will fulfill what was commanded them;
and all the sons of earth will seek to hide themselves from
the presence of the Great Glory,
and they will be shaken and tremble.
And you, sinners, will be cursed forever;
you will have no peace.

---

a Two lines follow restored Gk: Eth mss vary. See *1 Enoch 1*, 505.

b Text of vv 1c-3c in disarray in Gk and Eth. For reconstruction see *1 Enoch 1*,
505.

Enoch's Sixth Discourse: A Disputation on Justice and the Judgment (102:4—104:8)

An Exhortation to the Righteous Dead

4   Fear not, souls of the righteous;
            take courage, you pious who have died.[a]

5   And do not grieve because your souls have descended into
            Sheol with grief,
            and your body of flesh did not fare in your life according
            to your piety,
            because the days that you lived[b] were days of sinners and
            curses on the earth.

6   When you die, then the sinners say about you,
       "The pious have died according to fate,[c]
            and what have they gained from their deeds?

7   Look, then, how they die in grief and darkness,[d]
            and what advantage do they have over us?

8   Henceforth let them arise and be saved,
            and they shall forever see <the light>.[e]
       But, look, they have died,
            and henceforth (and) forever they will not see the light.

9   Therefore it is good for us to eat and drink,
            to plunder and sin and steal
            and get wealth and see good days.[f]

10   Look, then, those who consider themselves righteous[g]—of
            what sort their destruction has been—
            no righteousness[h] was found in them until they died.

11   And they perished and became as those who are not,
            and their souls descended with pain into Sheol."

---

a For the textual complexities, see *1 Enoch 1*, 513.

b Emending Gk *ēte* (*you were*, also Eth) to *zēte*.

c Eth *as we die*. See *1 Enoch 1*, 519–20.

d For textual problems, see *1 Enoch 1*, 513.

e Added by analogy with v 8d.

f For the textual problems in these three lines, see *1 Enoch 1*, 513–14.

g Gk with lacuna filled: Eth *the righteous*.

h Gk: Eth *unrighteousness*.

103:1   And now I swear to you, the righteous, by the glory of the
            Great One,
            and by his splendid kingship and his majesty I swear to
            you[a]
2   that I know this mystery.
            For I have read the tablets of heaven,
            and I have seen the writing of what must be,[b]
            and I know the things that are written in them and
            inscribed concerning you—
3   that good things and joy and honor have been prepared
            and written down for the souls of the pious who have
            died;
            and much good will be given to you in the place of your
            labors,
            and your lot will exceed the lot of the living.
4   The souls of the pious who have died will come to life,
            and they will rejoice and be glad;[c]
            and their spirits will not perish,
            nor their memory from the presence of the Great One
            for all the generations of eternity.
            Therefore, do not fear their reproaches.

A Woe Against the Dead Sinners

5   Woe to you, dead sinners.
            When you die in your sinful wealth,
            those who are like you say about you,
            "Blessed are the sinners
            all their days that they have seen.
6   And now they have died with goods and wealth,
            and affliction and murder they have not seen in their life.
            They have died in splendor,
            and judgment was not executed on them in their life."

---

a Wording of these two lines in Eth mss varies: Gk mainly lost in a lacuna.
b Gk lit. *writing of necessity*: Eth corrupt *holy writing* or *writing of the holy ones*.
c Gk omits *and be glad*.

7   Know that down to Sheol they will lead your souls;
            and there they will be in great distress,
8   and in darkness and in a snare and in a flaming fire.
        Into great judgment your souls will enter,
            and the great judgment will be[a]
            for all the generations of eternity.
        Woe to you, you will have no peace.

A Refutation of the Righteous Who Are Alive

9   Do not say, you who are righteous and pious in life,[b]
        "In the days of our tribulation, we toiled laboriously,
            and every tribulation we saw, and many evils we found.
        We were consumed and became few, and our spirits, small;
10   and we were destroyed and there was no one to help us
                with word and deed;
            we were powerless and found nothing.[c]
        We were crushed and destroyed,
            and we gave up hope any more to know safety from day to
                day;
11   we had hoped to be the head and became the tail.
        We toiled and labored and were not masters of our labor;
            we became the food of the sinners.
        The lawless weighed down their yoke upon us;
12   our enemies were our masters,
        they goaded us on and penned us in,[d]
            and to our enemies we bowed our necks,
            and they had no mercy on us.
13   We sought to get away from them,
            so that we might escape and be refreshed;
            but we found no place to flee and be safe from them.

---

a Gk omits clause, which may be a double reading in Eth.
b Eth *Do not say to the righteous and pious who are in life.*
c For the textual complexities in Gk and Eth, see *1 Enoch 1*, 514.
d For the textual problems in Gk and Eth, see *1 Enoch 1*, 514–15.

14   We complained to the rulers in our tribulation,
    and cried out against those who struck us down and
        oppressed us;[a]
  but our complaints they did not receive,
    nor did they wish to give a hearing to our voice.
15   They did not help us,
    they did not find (anything) against those who oppressed
        us and devoured us.[b]
  But they strengthened against us
    them who killed us and made us few.
  They did not disclose their iniquities,
    nor did they remove from us the yoke of them who
        devoured us and dispersed us and murdered us.
  They did not disclose concerning those who murdered us,
    nor did they make mention that they raised their hands
        against us."[c]
104:1   I swear to you that the angels in heaven make mention of
    you for good before the glory of the Great One,
    and your names are written before the glory of the Great
        One,
2   Take courage, then;[d]
    for formerly you were worn out by evils and tribulations,
    but now you will shine like the luminaries of heaven;
    you will shine and appear,[e]
    and the portals of heaven will be opened for you.
3   Your cry will be heard,
    and the judgment for which you cry will also appear to
        you.[f]

---

a Eth *and devoured us*. For both verbs, cf. v 15b.
b Eth of these two lines shorter and apparently defective.
c Eth: Gk appears to be corrupt here.
d Eth *Be hopeful*.
e Two verbs could be translation variants of Aram.
f For the textual problems in vv 3-6, see *1 Enoch 1*, 515.

    For from the rulers inquiry will be made concerning your
        tribulation,
      and from all who helped them who oppressed you and
        devoured you, (inquiry will be made) regarding your
        evils.

4   Take courage and do not abandon your hope,
      for you will have great joy like the angels of heaven.

5   And what will you have to do?
     You will not have to hide on the day of the great judgment,
      and you will not be found as the sinners,
      and the great judgment will be (far) from you
      for all the generations of eternity.

6   Fear not, O righteous, when you see the sinners growing
        strong and prospering,
      and do not be their companions;
    but stay far from all their iniquities,
      for you will be companions of the host of heaven.

A Refutation of the Sinners Who Are Alive

7   Do not say, O sinners,[a]
     "None of our sins will be searched out and written down."
     All your sins are being written down day by day.

8   And now I show you that light and darkness, day and night,
      observe all your sins.

Conclusion to the Epistle (104:9—105:2)

104:9   Do not err in your hearts or lie,
      or alter the words of truth,
      or falsify the words of the Holy One,
      or give praise to your errors.
    For it is not to righteousness that all your lies and all your
      error lead, but to great sin.

---

a Emending Gk *Do not say that sinners* in analogy to 102:4. See *1 Enoch 1*, 515.

10   And now I know this mystery,
            that sinners will alter and copy the words of truth,
                and pervert many and lie and invent great fabrications,
                and write books in their own names.
11   Would that they would write all my words in truth,[a]
            and neither remove nor alter these words,
             but write in truth all that I testify to them.
12   And again I know a second mystery,
            that to the righteous and pious and wise
                my books will be given for the joy of righteousness and
                    much wisdom.
13   Indeed, to them the books will be given,[b]
            and they will believe in them,
                and in them all the righteous will rejoice and be glad,
                to learn from them all the paths of truth.[c]
105:1   In those days, says the Lord, they will summon and testify
                against[d] the sons of earth in their wisdom.
            Instruct them, for you are their leaders and . . . rewards[e] over
                all the earth.
2   For I and my son will join ourselves with them forever in the
                paths of truth in their life.
            And you will have peace.
            Rejoice, O children of truth. Amen.

---

  a Gk Eth add *in their names, in their tongues,* an evident dittograph from previous
line.
  b Gk omits the line.
  c Chapter 105 omitted in Gk, due to hmt. Some form of it is attested in fragmentary Aram.
  d Or *to.*
  e Wording here is uncertain. Text may be defective.

The Birth of Noah

(Chapters 106–107)

106:1   After a time, I took a wife for Methuselah my son, and she bore a son and called his name Lamech. Righteousness was brought low until that day.

And when (Lamech) had come of age, he took for himself a wife, and she conceived from him and bore a child. 2/ And when the child was born,[a] his body was whiter than snow and redder than a rose, his hair was all white and like white wool and curly. Glorious <was his face>.[b] When he opened his eyes, the house shone like the sun. 3/ And he stood up from the hands of the midwife, and he opened his mouth and praised the Lord <of eternity>.[c]

4   And Lamech was afraid of him, and he fled and came to Methuselah his father. 5/ And he said to him, "A strange child has been born to me. He is not like human beings, but (like) the sons of the angels of heaven. His form is strange, not like us. His eyes are like the rays of the sun, and glorious is his face. 6/ I think that he is not from me, but from the angels. And I fear him, lest something happen in his days on the earth. 7/ I beg you, father, and beseech you, go to Enoch our father and learn the truth from him, for his dwelling is with the angels."

---

a Eth omits the clause. The poetic structure evident in the parallel vv 10-12 is not so evident here in vv 2-6.

b *his face* supplied by analogy with v 5.

c Phrase omitted in Gk and different in Eth, supplied by analogy with v 11 with a similar expression in the Latin text.

8   When Methuselah heard the words of his son, he came to me
at the ends of the earth, where he heard I was then. And he
said to me, "My father, hear my voice and come to me."[a]
And I heard his voice and came to him and said, "Look, here
I am, child. Why have you come to me, child?"

9   He answered and said,
"Because of great distress I have come to you,
   and because of a terrible vision I have approached here,
     father.[b]

10   And now, my father, hear me,
for a child has been born to Lamech my son,
   and his form and appearance are not like the form of
     human beings.
And his color is whiter than snow and redder than a rose,
   and the hair of his head is whiter than white wool.
And his eyes are like the rays of the sun,
   and he opened his eyes and made the whole house bright.

11   And he stood up from the hands of the midwife,
   and he opened his mouth and praised the Lord of
     eternity.[c]

12   And Lamech my son was afraid
   and he fled to me.
He does not believe that (the child) is his son,
   but that (he is) from the angels of heaven.
And, look, I have come to you,
   because from the angels you have the exact facts and the
     truth."

13   Then I, Enoch, answered and said,
"The Lord will renew his commandment upon the earth,
   just as, child, I have seen and told you.

---

a Eth omits the quotation and has *cried* for *said.*

b On the text of these two lines, see *1 Enoch 1,* 537.

c Eth *Lord of heaven*: Latin as in v 3.

That in the generation of Jared, my father, †they transgressed
    the word of the Lord/the covenant of heaven†,[a]

14   and look, they went on sinning and transgressing the
      custom.
With women they were mingling,
    and with them they were sinning.
They married some of them,
    and they went on begetting (children), not like spirits, but
    of flesh.

15   And there will be great wrath upon the earth and a flood,
    and there will be great destruction for a year.

16   And this child that was born to you will be left on the earth,
    and his three children will be saved with him,
    when all people on the earth die.

17   And he will cleanse[b] the earth from the corruption that is on
    it.

18   And now tell Lamech,
'He is your child in truth,
    and <this child will be righteous and>[c] blameless,
<And "Noah"> call his name,
    for he will be your remnant,
    from whom you will find rest.'
He and his sons will be saved from the corruption of the
    earth
    and from all sins and from all iniquities that are consum-
    mated on the earth in his days.

19   And after this there will be stronger iniquity than that which
    was formerly consummated on the earth. (For I know the
    mysteries <of the Lord>[d] that the holy ones have revealed and
    shown to me, and that I have read in the tablets of heaven.

---

a Either there is a double reading here that derives from alternative translations of
Aram, or a verb has dropped from the text. See *1 Enoch 1*, 538 for the confused textual
evidence.

b Emending Gk *praunei* (*soothe, tame*) to *plynei*, following Eth.

c For this emendation of the Gk, see *1 Enoch 1*, 538–39.

d For this emendation, see *1 Enoch 1*, 539.

107:1   And I have seen written in them that generation upon gen-
        eration will do evil in this way,[a]
            and the evil will be until there arise generations of righ-
            teousness.)
        And evil and wickedness will end,
            and violence will cease from the earth,
            and good things will come upon the earth to them.
2   Now go, child, and tell Lamech your son that this child that
        has been born is his child, truly and without deception."
3   When Methuselah heard the words of Enoch his father—
        for (Enoch) revealed them to him secretly—(Methuselah)
        returned and revealed everything to (Lamech).
        And his name was called Noah—
            he who gladdens the earth from destruction.[b]

---

a Text for the rest of the chapter based in part on Aram. See *1 Enoch 1*, 539.
b Gk adds (*the*) *Epistle of Enoch*, a subscript.

A Final Book by Enoch

(Chapter 108)

108:1   ANOTHER BOOK THAT ENOCH WROTE for his son Methuselah and for those who would come after him and keep the law in the last days.

2   You who have observed (it) and**ᵃ** are waiting in these days until the evildoers are brought to an end and the power of the sinners is brought to an end— 3/ you wait until sin passes away.

For their names will be erased from the book of life and from the books of the holy ones,**ᵇ**
and their descendants will perish forever;
their spirits will be slaughtered,
and they will cry out and groan in a desolate, unseen place,
and in fire they will burn, for there is no earth there.

4   I saw there something like a cloud, which could not be discerned, since because of its depth I was unable to look up at it. And flames of fire I saw burning gloriously, and something like glorious mountains were turning over and quaking to and fro.

5   And I asked one of the holy angels who were with me, "What is this glorious (place), for there is no heaven, but only flames of fire that are burning and the sound of weeping and crying and groaning and severe pain."

6   And he said to me, "The place that you see—here are thrown the spirits of the sinners and blasphemers and those who do evil and those who alter everything that the Lord has said

---

a Five mss omit *and.*

b Mss differ as to which books are meant. See *1 Enoch 1*, 552.

by the mouth of the prophets (about) the things that will be
done.

7   For there are books and records about them in heaven
above,
so that the angels may read them
and know what will happen to the sinners and the spirits
of the humble,
and those who afflicted their bodies, and were recompensed
by God;
and those who were abused by evil men;

8   those who love God,
and do not love gold and silver and all the good things
that are in the world;
but gave their bodies to torment;

9   and those who from the time they existed did not desire the
food that is in the world,
but considered themselves as a breath that passes away;
and to this they kept.
The Lord tested them much,
and their spirits were found pure,
so that they might bless his name.

10   And all their blessings I have recounted in the books.
And he has recompensed them for their lives,
for these were found to have loved heaven
more than their life that is in the world.[a]
Although they were trampled down by evil men and heard
reproach and insult from them and were abused,
yet they blessed me.

11   And now I will summon the spirits of the pious (who are)
from the generation of light;
and I will transform those who <have descended into>[b]
darkness,
who in their bodies were not recompensed with the honor
appropriate to their faithfulness.

---

a All but one ms read *everlasting life*. Reading of the one ms followed above, parallels the expression in vv 8b and 9a.

b Emending *tawaldu* (*were born* [*in*]) to *waradu*. Cf. 102:7.

12   Indeed, I will bring forth in shining light those who loved
             my holy name,
          and I will seat each one on the throne of his honor,
13   and they will shine for times without number.
        For righteous is the judgment of God,
             and to the faithful he shows faithfulness,
             because they abide in the paths of truth.
14   And the righteous, as they shine, will see those who were
             born in darkness cast into darkness;
15   and the sinners will cry out and see them shining;
          and they, for their part, will depart to where the days and
             times are written for them.

2013. 09. 06   18.00 (14.50)